T0330533

A Critical History of the Economy

Drawing on recent debates in critical international political economy (IPE), this book mobilizes the idea that the economy does not exist separately from society and politics to develop a detailed intellectual history of how the economy came to be seen as an independent domain.

In contrast to typical approaches to writing the history of economic thought, which assume the reality of the economy, the author describes the forms of intellectual argument that made it possible to conceive of the national and international economies as objects of intellectual inquiry. At the centre of this process was the analytical separation of power and wealth. Walter thus offers a broad historical perspective on the emergence of current IPE theory, while linking the field with contextual intellectual history.

This important and innovative volume will be of strong interest to students and scholars of international political economy, international relations, economics, history, and political theory.

Ryan Walter is Lecturer in the School of Politics and International Relations at the Australian National University. His research interests focus on the history of economic and political thought.

RIPE Series in Global Political Economy

This series, published in association with the *Review of International Political Economy*, provides a forum for current and interdisciplinary debates in international political economy. The series aims to advance understanding of the key issues in the global political economy, and to present innovative analyses of emerging topics. The titles in the series focus on three broad themes:

- the structures, processes and actors of contemporary global transformations;
- the changing forms taken by governance, at scales from the local and everyday to the global and systemic;
- the inseparability of economic from political, social and cultural questions, including resistance, dissent and social movements.

The series comprises two strands:

The *RIPE Series in Global Political Economy* aims to address the needs of students and teachers, and the titles will be published in hardback and paperback. Titles include:

Transnational Classes and International Relations
Kees van der Pijl

Gender and Global Restructuring
Sightings, sites and resistances
Edited by Marianne H. Marchand and Anne Sisson Runyan

Global Political Economy
Contemporary theories
Edited by Ronen Palan

Ideologies of Globalization
Contending visions of a new world order
Mark Rupert

The Clash within Civilisations
Coming to terms with cultural conflicts
Dieter Senghaas

Global Unions?
Theory and strategies of organized labour in the global political economy
Edited by Jeffrey Harrod and Robert O'Brien

Political Economy of a Plural World
Critical reflections on power, morals and civilizations
Robert Cox with Michael Schechter

A Critical Rewriting of Global Political Economy
Integrating reproductive, productive and virtual economies
V. Spike Peterson

Contesting Globalization
Space and place in the world economy
André C. Drainville

Global Institutions and Development
Framing the world?
Edited by Morten Bøås and Desmond McNeill

Global Institutions, Marginalization and Development
Craig N. Murphy

Critical Theories, International Relations and 'the Anti-Globalisation Movement'
The politics of global resistance
Edited by Catherine Eschle and Bice Maiguashca

Globalization, Governmentality and Global Politics
Regulation for the rest of us?
Ronnie D. Lipschutz with James K. Rowe

Critical Perspectives on Global Governance
Rights and regulation in governing regimes
Jean Grugel and Nicola Piper

Beyond States and Markets
The challenges of social reproduction
Edited by Isabella Bakker and Rachel Silvey

The Industrial Vagina
The political economy of the global sex trade
Sheila Jeffreys

Capital as Power
A study of order and creorder
Jonathan Nitzan and Shimshon Bichler

The Global Political Economy of Intellectual Property Rights, Second Edition
The new enclosures
Christopher May

Corporate Power and Ownership in Contemporary Capitalism
The politics of resistance and domination
Susanne Soederberg

Savage Economics
Wealth, poverty and the temporal walls of capitalism
David L. Blaney and Naeem Inayatullah

Cultural Political Economy
Edited by Jacqueline Best and Matthew Paterson

Gender and Global Restructuring Second Edition
Sightings, sites and resistances
Edited by Marianne H. Marchand and Anne Sisson Runyan

Routledge/RIPE Studies in Global Political Economy is a forum for innovative new research intended for a high-level specialist readership, and the titles will be available in hardback only. Titles include:

* Also available in paperback

A Critical History of the Economy

On the birth of the national and international economies

Ryan Walter

Routledge
Taylor & Francis Group

LONDON AND NEW YORK

First published 2011
by Routledge
2 Park Square, Milton Park, Abingdon, Oxon, OX14 4RN

Simultaneously published in the USA and Canada
by Routledge
270 Madison Avenue, New York, NY 10016

Routledge is an imprint of the Taylor & Francis Group, an Informa business

British Library Cataloguing in Publication Data
A catalogue record for this book is available from the British Library

Library of Congress Cataloging in Publication Data
Walter, Ryan.
    A critical history of the economy: on the birth of the national
    and international economies/Ryan Walter.
        p. cm. – (RIPE series in global political economy; 34)
    1. Economics–History. 2. International trade–History.
    I. Title.
HB75.W352 2011
330.9–dc22   2011005971

ISBN: 978-0-415-58890-4 (hbk)
ISBN: 978-0-203-80611-1 (ebk)

Typeset in Times New Roman by Sunrise Setting Ltd, Torquay, UK

For JMW and WCW

Contents

Acknowledgements

Writing the acknowledgements for a book reveals how many debts are incurred in the process. My greatest is to Barry Hindess, who supervised the doctoral thesis this work grew out of, and patiently imparted the rich and incisive thinking for which he is known. Friends and colleagues at the Australian National University were also invaluable sources of dialogue and encouragement, and Michael Leininger-Ogawa and David West deserve special thanks for this. My former home, at the Centre for the History of European Discourses at the University of Queensland, proved both stimulating and collegial. In particular, Ian Hunter freely gave time and effort to help me think through the argument, and this has resulted in some of the major claims being recast in a stronger form. Chiara Beccalossi and Marina Bollinger were regular interlocutors, while Philip Almond and Peter Cryle gave helpful advice. Several colleagues outside the Centre lent support to this project: Ian Cook, Richard Devetak, David Eden, David Martin Jones, Gavin Kendall, Alison Scott, and Gary Wickham all have my thanks. Keith Tribe has remained a distant but generous correspondent after examining my doctoral thesis. His work is the basic building block for this research, as anyone who is familiar with it will see, and I am also grateful for having such a model of scholarship to try to emulate. Carolina Caliaba Crespo edited the manuscript with her usual dedication and flair, and she also dissuaded the author from doubt and despair at key moments. The RIPE series editors nurtured the project through criticisms and suggestions, and I am especially indebted to Paul Langley, who supported the idea from the beginning. Finally, earlier versions of parts of the argument were developed in seminar presentations at the Australian National University and the University of Queensland, and in journal articles in *Economy and Society*, *History of European Ideas*, and *Review of International Studies*. I am indebted to all of these forums for spurring my thinking.

Ryan Walter
The Australian National University

Note on the text

The original spelling, capitalization, italicization, and punctuation have been retained when quoting from primary sources. In those cases where the original date of publication is different to the date of the version quoted from, the original is provided in square brackets. Gendered language has been used in relation to primary texts, and this is intended to convey their original meaning.

Introduction

The national economy and the international economy are two nominal objects that at once underwrite and are the targets of a host of governmental programmes and desires. We associate management of the national economy with government budgets and central banks, while international economic governance is shaped by inter-governmental bodies such as the World Trade Organization and the International Monetary Fund. These practices and institutions are central to contemporary political life, and it is therefore no surprise that the nature and purpose of the national and international economies have been formulated in diverse doctrines, from fascism to free trade, and subjected to fierce political contest. This book describes the historical emergence of the domestic and international economies as independent intellectual objects. More specifically, it investigates how the domestic economy came to be seen as a domain separate from the state, and how the international economy came to be seen as possessing its own self-regulating nature independent of the governmental actions of sovereign states.

The book thus offers an intellectual history of early modern British economic thought, from approximately 1650 to 1820. As the title indicates, our task is to provide a critical history of these domains of the economic, and since 'critical' is a contested term, whoever uses it is obliged to explain what they mean. In short, our account is critical because the economy is treated as something that emerges from reciprocal relations between forms of economic argument and economic practices – markets, exchanges, national planning, global dependencies – that are shaped by these forms of argument. We can therefore approach those ideas, governmental programmes, and everyday practices that we are accustomed to calling economic as forming a nominal field of action – the economy. This involves suspending the question of the truth or falsity of present and past doctrines about the nature of the economy, because these doctrines represent a crucial element of the economic field we are attempting to account for historically.

This critical approach contrasts with the more usual method of investigation, which is to treat the economy as a pre-given referent that exists naturally as part of the furniture of the world. This presupposition enables the correspondence between economic ideas and economic reality to be narrated in terms of the rise of economic science. The resulting narratives tend to exhibit both *progressivism* (economic science comes to capture economic phenomena with increasing accuracy) and *naturalism* (the economy exists independently of our practices of accumulating knowledge about its workings). Such an approach bears two heavy historiographical burdens. The first, which is a direct consequence of progressivism, is that early modern writings on trade, money, and so on are viewed as primitive versions of economics. This viewpoint assumes that our modern economic questions are perennial, which forecloses the possibility of learning whether earlier European societies formulated different questions regarding commerce and wealth, to which they gave answers that are not readily assimilated to our conception of the economy. The second burden, which follows from naturalism, is to presuppose that there are things in the world that are economic in essence, such as labour, trade, and money. This presupposition blocks access to investigating how the economy was delineated as an object of thought, which in turn prevents us from asking a whole array of intellectual-historical questions regarding the relations between forms of economic thought and types of economic practice.

These abstract claims about historiography can be fleshed out with reference to a familiar example. The notion of the disembedded economy was developed by Karl Polanyi in his celebrated book, *The Great Transformation: The Political and Economic Origins of Our Time*, and in his subsequent work. The disembedding of the economy referred to the rise of a utopian project in the West from the turn of the nineteenth century. This project sought to alter institutional relations between the economy and society, in essence, 'instead of economy being embedded in social relations, social relations are embedded in the economic system' (Polanyi 2001: 60).

As the subtitle of Polanyi's book suggests, describing the attempted disembedding of the economy and its consequences bears a similarity to the task assumed by this study. The fundamental difference is that Polanyi did not take the economy to be a nominal field, but he instead treated it as a natural category. We are told that the economic denotes 'man's dependence for his living upon nature and his fellows. It refers to the interchange with his natural and social environment, in so far as this results in supplying him with the means of material want satisfaction' (Polanyi 1957a: 243).

Here we can see how Polanyi deduced the category of the economic from a philosophical anthropology of humanity's material needs, and this means that, just like our dependence on nature, the economic is timeless. The economy could, however, be institutionally integrated with everyday life in different modes, in particular: reciprocity, redistribution, and exchange (ibid.: 250–2). The institutional connections between the economy and society were typically dominated by one of these three modes, and each had different consequences for how society was organized and how the economy was perceived.

Polanyi maintained that when reciprocity and redistribution were the dominant forms of integration between economy and society, there were no specifically economic institutions, such as markets. The economic process consequently 'runs in the grooves of different structures', such as family, politics, and religion. In a society where the economy was institutionally embedded in this way, 'no concept of an economy need arise', because it was 'almost impossible for the observer to collect the fragments of the economic process and piece them together'. Correspondingly, 'his emotions fail to convey any experience that he could identify as "economic"' (Polanyi 1957b: 70–1). This claim presumes a correspondence between economic ideas and economic reality.

Polanyi's account was also informed by teleology, for it posited an inevitable clash between economy and society. We are told that the rise of the market economy was significant because it represented the only form of economy that attempted to dominate society institutionally: a 'self-regulating market demands nothing less than the institutional separation of society into an economic and a political sphere'. By contrast, traditionally the economic order was 'merely a function of the social order' (Polanyi 2001: 74). This is the context for Polanyi's famous double movement thesis, which stated that the spread of market organization gave rise to a response from society to protect itself by insulating certain commodities – land, labour, and money – from market logic. These commodities were so intimately tied to social existence that to subject them to the market mechanism would result in the destruction of society; the varieties of protectionism were therefore instances of society's defensive reflexes (ibid.: 74–80).

One problem here is that, in hindsight, the clash between the economy and society that Polanyi described in the 1940s did not have the definitive character he imbued it with. The self-regulating market did not fade as an ideal but was powerfully reasserted by renovated forms of utopian economic argument in the 1970s and 1980s.[1] A second and related issue is the philosophical character of the projected economy–society contest,[2] for this framing leads us away from investigating how economic phenomena were abstracted away from the terrain of state administration and collected together as economic in the first place. In short, we find that the context for this process was shifts in specific genres of intellectual argument: counsel on trade and its outgrowth, political economy. Thus, the virtue of intellectual history is to make it possible to examine theoretical argument (and its effects) in an historical-empirical manner. The result of our critical history is therefore not to provide an historical-theoretical rationale for embedding the economy in society. Rather, the effects of our history are these: first, to de-naturalize a split that is routinely taken for granted in the question of how the state should regulate the economy, and, second, to underscore the effects of theoretical argument in demarcating unities such as state, society, and economy, which may then feature as the targets of governmental action and philosophical histories alike.

In focusing on the role of economic argument in shaping governmental action, this book intersects with recent research in political economy that has examined the role of rhetoric, norms, and the performativity of economic science in governing economic behaviour. Jason Sharman's study of disputes between the Organisation for Economic Co-operation and Development (OECD) and non-member states over tax reform, for example, described how rhetoric and reputation became determining factors in a contest that one might normally expect to have been decided by the material might of the OECD and its member states

(Sharman 2006). Analogously, by treating capital mobility as a policy norm, Rawi Abdelal revised the usual globalization narrative that centres American hegemony and instead highlighted the leading role of European policy-makers (Abdelal 2007). Rodney Bruce Hall similarly challenged the image of central banking as a technical activity by revealing its dependence on 'social facts' and rule-governed behaviour (Hall 2008). Finally, Michel Callon's work invites us to understand economics as performing the economy. He mobilized this premise through a number of concepts, such as economization (marking an entity as economic in nature) and framing (directing agents towards a particular cultural frame to enable calculation), and these concepts were intended to illuminate the processes that format economic life (Çalışkan and Callon 2009; Callon 1998). While each of these contributions is distinctive, they all eschewed a comfortable split between economic reality and representations of economic reality. This is also the guiding premise for the intellectual history that follows.

The merits of intellectual history for political economy – the history of economic thought in particular – have recently been demonstrated by Marieke de Goede's genealogy of finance from the early modern period to contemporary markets, and by Donald MacKenzie's study of the development of late twentieth-century finance theory and its interpenetration with financial markets (de Goede 2005; MacKenzie 2006). Both histories revealed the powerful effects of economic argument in organizing and governing parts of everyday life. As we have seen, it is this move – suspending the naturalness of a nominal domain such as finance – that is the key to producing critical histories. Yet we need to distinguish between strands of the recent historical turn in political economy. In particular, a few words should be said about the influential version articulated by Matthew Watson, which is centred on the claim that classical political economy can act as a store of theoretical resources for contemporary theorizing (Watson 2005). More specifically, classical political economy is said to offer the tools necessary to apprehend the economy as an historical and social process. Without denying its value for this theoretical task, Watson's approach to intellectual history ultimately inhibits historical understanding, since a bygone tradition is constructed to perform rhetorical services in the present, namely, providing a pedigree for a rival framework to neoclassical economics. Watson's approach therefore represents progressivism in reverse: the yardstick for assessing economic thought is not the usual neoclassical economics but the predecessor it is seen to have vanquished in the late nineteenth century – classical political economy.

Given that there are different styles of intellectual history, it is worth indicating the sources for the critical approach developed here. The immediate methodological inspiration derives from Michel Foucault's studies of the formation of nominal objects, such as sexuality and madness (Foucault 1990, 2006). Foucault's decisive claim was that 'things' such as sexuality are not pre-given but are formed from practices of knowing (theology, psychoanalysis, sexology) and practices of governing (confession, therapy).[3] Foucault did not produce a dedicated work on economics, but he did offer some provocative insights in his archaeology of the human sciences (Foucault 2002), and in his work on governmentality (Foucault

2007, 2008). In the latter works, political economy was portrayed as central to the emergence of liberal techniques of government in the West for a complex set of reasons, the most important of which was that political economy freed the art of government from its moorings in sovereignty. While Foucault's account is deeply influential for the work at hand, it is nevertheless revised in some important respects in what follows.[4]

A second line of influence is Keith Tribe's histories of economic discourse in the British and German contexts (Tribe 1978, 1988, 1995a). In the British setting, as Tribe demonstrated so powerfully, the discourse of political œconomy was displaced by political economy around the turn of the nineteenth century. Political œconomy imagined the state as an enlarged royal household, and it was succeeded by a discourse that investigated the laws of production and distribution governing a national economy. Tribe's account provides a key source for our study, but it is inflected to focus on the modalities of state power, and extended to take account of the international context of state administration.

The third source drawn on is the contextual approach to the history of political thought associated with the 'Cambridge School', and within it the work of J. G. A. Pocock and Quentin Skinner in particular (see Pocock 2009; Skinner 2002: Vol. I). One of the axioms developed in contextual scholarship is that it is necessary to ask what a given author was *doing* when they wrote in a certain historical situation: for example, advising a prince, attacking the Church's jurisdiction, or designing a constitution to safeguard a polity's virtue. Identifying a writer's specific task lends concrete guidance to the investigation of textual meaning in a way that overly capacious categories such as 'political philosophy' or 'economics' do not. This concern will direct our inquiry at key moments, but the equally distinctive contextual concern with the languages and vocabularies of intellectual argument will be less in evidence. The reason is that the key languages that have guided contextual study of economic thought, in particular, civic humanism and natural law, are languages that primarily related to legitimizing rule over a polity and the moral personality of citizen-subjects. As John Brewer noted in his landmark account of state power, legitimacy relates to only one face of the early modern British state, and it has led attention away from the other, the outward facing fiscal-military state that mobilized extraordinary resources to make war in a threatening world of rival states (Brewer 1990: xvii–xviii; see also Brewer 1994: 56). As numerous scholars have demonstrated, commerce was talked about in the languages of civic virtue, law, and their syntheses; the choice of language typically betrayed (and shaped) a preference for one type of polity over another.[5] This insight is indispensable. We need to know, however, whether commerce was being talked about in relation to the state or the economy. It is therefore necessary to distinguish between two processes: the shift from state to economy as the object of discourse and, on the other hand, the eclipse of civic humanist and republican modes of thought by liberal modes. As we shall see, these occurred in different historical contexts.[6]

To answer this question, our inquiry will be based on the notion of forms of argument, an approach implicit in Tribe's work (Tribe 1978), which essentially asks two empirical questions. First, how are arguments about commerce, trade, money, labour, and so on constructed? Second, does this form of argument make the economy cognizable as an object distinct from the state, in the case of the national economy, or as an object distinct from the actions of states, in the case of the international economy? What needs to be emphasized is that it is certain forms of argument that make the economy cognizable, for this is the sharp edge of the critical methodological stricture that directs us not to treat the economy as a natural object that is simply 'perceived' by a subject.

A useful analogy here is with Ludwig Wittgenstein's claim that it was misleading to 'talk of thinking as of a "mental activity"', as 'thinking is essentially the *activity* of operating with signs' (Wittgenstein 1958a: 6; emphasis added). A good example is the expansion of an arithmetic series using an algebraic formula. Consider the equation $Yn = 5n + 5$. Starting from $n = 1$, and following the sequence of natural numbers, the series 10, 15, 20... is obtained. It is not that a student learns to 'think' these numbers, but rather that they learn to produce the series through operating the numbers and symbols of the formula. It is not abstract thought that is at work but the concrete and particular activity of expanding a number series (see Wittgenstein 1958b: 59–61). The analogy leads us to reject the idea that one simply 'thinks' the economy in favour of recognizing that to describe economic relations of production and distribution through specific forms of argument is also an activity, one only performed by certain agents under specific historical conditions. One of the effects of performing this activity is that it becomes possible to cognize the economy as a distinct sphere, which then underwrites a host of governmental programmes targeted at this sphere.

It is the history of these forms of argument and their effects that we will examine in what follows. The notion of forms of argument and their effects is a more specialized tool than the Cambridge School investigation of languages, and this reflects our focus on the emergence of the economy as an object of thought, a focus that will enable us to cover the sweep of chronology necessary to the investigation. As this last claim suggests, the history that follows does not pretend to completeness but only seeks to indicate a critical approach to making the economy intelligible historically. With these points in mind we can preview the contours of the study.

Structure of the argument

The argument is divided into three parts. Part I establishes two key aspects of the intellectual context in early modern Britain. The first is the practice of providing counsel to statesmen, which was both a central presupposition of intellectual argument and subject to contest. Counsel could be perceived as intruding on state prerogative, while deafness on the part of rulers could be portrayed as tyranny. This picture is complicated by the fact that counsel had both implicit and explicit audiences, so that while a statesman might be the stated addressee, the intended target was also a broad counselling public that included merchants and projectors. Focusing on this aspect of the intellectual milieu goes some distance to satisfying the contextual concern that we recover what it is these writers were doing when they wrote on topics such as trade. The second step towards understanding the intellectual context is to identify three genres of counsel – the analysis of interest, political arithmetic, and counsel on trade – and then understand how these genres were related to each other.

These two preliminary steps make it possible to resist the progressive impulse to view counsel on trade in terms of chronology – and hence as a seventeenth-century anticipation of economics – and instead characterize this genre as a species of counsel that bore certain relations with neighbouring genres. Attention shifts in Part II to this genre's typical forms of argument and the objects counsellors on trade could cognize by using these arguments. The key to this reconstruction is the pre-eminence given to the state's need to grow in strength and wealth in order to survive in a world where state competition and warfare were endemic. Counsel on trade was therefore tethered to state administration, and in this connection we observe that strength and wealth were analysed in tandem. This collocation has profound significance for understanding the genre, for the accumulation of wealth could not be separated from the concern with state strength, or with the strength of international friends and enemies, except by novel arguments. Thus, the central claim advanced in Part II is that the forms of argument characteristic of counsel on trade did not make the national economy or the international economy cognizable in anything like our contemporary senses. These arguments did, however, represent processes of trade and exchange with a measure of complexity and intractability to state control, and this tension was a defining feature of counsel on trade. These forms of argument appear exotic to the contemporary student of international relations because they fused together trade and security, whereas today's conundrum is typically seen as being how to conceive of the interconnections between these two phenomena, usually via one elaboration or another of the states and markets pair.[7]

Part III describes how counsel on trade was altered by the forms of argument advanced by Adam Smith and David Ricardo. The first crucial break resulted from Smith's use of the accumulation of productive labour to ground the assessment of trade legislation, which acted as an analytical wedge between strength and wealth. Despite this important break, Smith's arguments remained imbricated in state administration and did not delineate the economy as a distinct, self-sustaining domain. This is exactly the effect of Ricardo's arguments, however, which established an abstract analysis of distribution. In this form, political economy set itself a narrow range of questions and addressed them with an equally narrow apparatus. As for the international economy, Smith's arguments produced an analysis of international trade that made it possible to assess the actions of states on the basis of their effects on the world's wealth. This analysis was then projected into historical time to endow the world economy with a *telos*. Although Ricardo's arguments regarding international trade differed from Smith's, they nevertheless made it possible for the political economist to accede to the international economy as an object of inquiry distinct from geo-politics. This troubled intellectual split between economics and power remains central to contemporary political economy, and this point closes the study.

Part I
Context

1 Counsellors to government

As part of our attempt to forestall treating the concerns of contemporary eco-nomics as natural and perennial, we need to investigate what earlier writers thought they were doing when writing on topics such as money and wealth. We can take an important step in this direction by paying attention to the practices and conceptions of counselling that typified early modern England. The key point to make in this regard is that counsel on trade was organized around two discursive figures: the counsellor who gave counsel, and the statesman who was projected as both the target of counsel and the agent capable of enacting the changes called for, whether by laws, policy, or good example. It is therefore necessary to distinguish between, on the one hand, the counsellor and statesman as tropes of argumen-tation and, on the other hand, the historical figures who actually counselled and conducted the business of government.

With this distinction in mind, we will be able to observe the range of histor-ical actors who proffered written counsel on trade and the various motives they appeared to have for doing so. It will also be possible to notice variation in how counsel on trade was elaborated, from William Cavendish's letter to the Prince of Wales to Nassau Senior's prospectus for a science remote from law-making. By paying attention to these changes in genre we not only can resist the unifying claims of progressive histories, but we will also be well placed to describe the effects of these changes in future chapters.

The rise of counselling

In the medieval period, addressing written counsel to the king was an established practice (Ferguson 1965: 3–41), and its place in English political thought was con-solidated by the arrival of Italian humanism. To simplify a complex process let us say that, under Henry VII and Henry VIII, the commercial gentry came to fill the ranks of the aristocracy as courtiers and statesmen, and this class used human-ist learning to distinguish themselves as ideally suited to assist in managing the affairs of state (Siegel 1952).[1] The core of humanism was the revival of classical Greek and Roman culture, especially with a view to the wisdom it contained for application in the present, and, by the time of Elizabeth I, humanist learning had become crucial for political advancement (Caspari 1954: 151–2). The venerable image that the new political advisers projected for themselves was the counsellor who had acquired classical learning for the purpose of engaging usefully in public affairs, a figure who thus reconciled the contesting classical ideals of the active life and the contemplative life (Skinner 1978: Vol. I: 213–21).[2]

By the mid-sixteenth century, counselling had become a central concept for imagining public life and justifying its institutions. Yet, as with most important concepts, it was subject to contest. A major fault-line lay between what we can call the sovereign and populist conceptions of counsel. On the sovereign under-standing, counsel was asked for by the monarch, who could then decline or accept it. Censorship could limit unwanted counsel, and punishment could deter: John Stubbs's right hand was cut off for impertinently advising against Elizabeth's proposed marriage to the Duke of Anjou (see Mears 2001).

The Privy Council was a select group of statesmen who initially met in the king's 'privy' apartments at court, and it sits nicely with this sovereign view (Elton 1953: 317–52; Guy 1995: 295, 305). The most powerful defence of the sovereign position came from Thomas Hobbes, whose Chapter 25, 'Of Counsell', began by distinguishing command from counsel: one is obliged to follow the former but not the latter, and the provocative implication was that, in a monarchy, Parliament only counsels. Hobbes also advised in favour of taking counsel from one person at a time to avoid advisers influencing each other and the formation of factions (Hobbes 1991 [1651]: 176–82). Hobbes's point was that counsel was not debate, and it was not directed to the political community to lend decisions legitimacy but to the sovereign to enable good laws.

By contrast, the institution of Parliament was aligned with the populist view of counsel, which saw counsel as essential to liberty and the justness of government, hence regular and orderly parliaments were a marker of freedom. The parliamen-tarians declared their purpose to be the removal of the king's bad counsel during the lead-up to the English Civil War, while they offered themselves as more worthy counsellors by the very fact of their position in Parliament, which they described as the realm's great council (see Condren 2006: 162–71).

Beyond these two institutional settings there was a wide range of subjects who also offered counsel through written advice openly addressed to officers of gov-ernment, such as parliamentarians and statesmen, while the implicit addressee was a broad readership composed of laymen, nobles, merchants, husbandmen, projec-tors, and administrators. Sir Thomas Smith identified this constituency when he welcomed not only learned men to give advice, but also merchants, husbandmen, and artificers, since 'every man is to be credited in that art that he is most exercised in' (Smith 1969 [1581]: 12). In this community of counsellors, we encounter both the self-interested pamphleteer who sought to promote legislation that would aid his private interests, and more publicly-spirited writers, whom Joseph Schumpeter called 'consultant administrators' (Schumpeter 1954a: 160). Both characteriza-tions can be apt for the same writer, who could also be a Member of Parliament or a courtier. The counsellor was a capacious figure, something we will come to see more clearly as we examine some of the addresses made by this figure's real-world counterparts who wrote on trade.

From counsel on trade to political economy

In seventeenth-century texts on trade, the counsellor functioned as a discursive figure, or an ideal type, who addressed their counsel to another discursive figure, the statesman. Together these two figures provided a frame for understanding the purpose of writing counsel and its connection with legislation and action: the knowing counsellor advised the statesman as to an ill and its remedy, or to the general nature of things in some domain, and the statesman could then make a remedial law, or execute a better general administration in the future. The concrete situation was usually not as neat as this, but it is important to note that sometimes it was.

One case where the figure of counsellor and its real-world correlate overlapped nicely was that of William Cavendish, who was, *inter alia*, a courtier and governor to Charles, Prince of Wales (later Charles II). Cavendish prepared a long letter of advice for Charles, claiming that it was 'written particularly for your Majesty when you are enthroned', but given to Charles earlier (perhaps 1659[3]). The printed text is just over one hundred pages long, and arranged into multiple categories, one of which is entitled 'For Trade'. Trade was described as 'an other Busines, then the Church, or the Lawe', and it was 'Imposible for any man, to bee A good states-man that doth not understand trade In some Measure' (Cavendish 1984 [1659]: 35, 38). The advice that Cavendish gave was typical for its time. Charles was advised, for example, to tend to his merchants because they enriched the country with trade and increased its shipping, which was a nursery for seamen and so strengthened the state's naval power. He was also told to check those trades that emptied the kingdom of its bullion, as the East Indian trade was said to do (ibid.: 36–9).

The relationship between counsellor and statesman was doubled in Francis Bacon's letter to the Duke of Buckingham, since Bacon (himself a counsellor and statesman) was counselling Buckingham, the favourite of James I, on how to be a good counsellor and intimate of the king. The central plank of Bacon's advice to Buckingham was to divide the petitions he received into groups according to the area of state business they related to, such as religion, law, war, and trade, and then seek further counsel himself from people learned in the relevant professions. Buckingham could then assess the advice he was given. In relation to trade, Bacon professed ignorance but then set out some received notions, such as discouraging luxuries but privileging those trades that set many hands to work (Bacon 1661: 5–6, 12–13). Bacon's trade maxims are only that, possessing the same rule-of-thumb character as Cavendish's despite the different mode of address. The point to note is that the figure of counsellor circulated quickly and easily, and it provided a discursive position from which to articulate advice on the government of trade.

The statesman was also an accommodating discursive figure, and so it is not necessary to suppose the king was the intended addressee. A good example is Josiah Child's pamphlet, *Brief Observations Concerning Trade*, the primary addressees of which were likely to have been statesmen other than the king. The pamphlet advanced several recommendations to restore England's trade, but it was mainly concerned with just one: lowering by law the maximum interest rate to 4 per cent (Child 1668). Child's pamphlet was circulated to Members of Parliament in 1665, published in 1668 when a Bill was before Parliament to reduce the interest rate, while his proposal was debated by a Lords' Committee on trade in 1669 (Letwin 1963: 5–6). We can therefore surmise that Child's arguments were intended to persuade these audiences of policy-makers (ibid.: 13), while his stated purpose for counselling was 'the good of my Native Country' (Child 1668: 18). The case of Child is instructive because it leads us to emphasize the figurative character of counsellor and statesman over the variable situation of the agents who mobilized these images.

Like Child, Nicholas Barbon claimed to serve the national interest by uncovering the nature of trade as a whole, as his compatriots had only managed to perceive the nature of particular parts, either from poor reasoning or private interest (Barbon 1690: Preface). This was a common enough tactic to differentiate one tract from another, and after revealing the workings of trade Barbon set out the implications for policy. We are told that 'Building is the chiefest Promoter of *Trade*', and for proof we need only look at the rich and powerful Dutch, who 'Incourage the Builder, and at the Charge of the *State*' (ibid.: 68). Nominating a particular trade as the most beneficial to the state and hence deserving special treatment in Barbon's fashion was a regular discursive move, but it looked bad for Barbon, who was a prominent builder in London (Letwin 1963: 49, 59).

The existence or perception of private interests of Barbon's kind, which could be served by the counsel being offered, was a sensitive issue. The prestige of the counsellor was dependent on their service to the public good, and the office was corrupted when it served the interests of a grasping merchant. Josiah Child's *Discourse About Trade* was published anonymously, no doubt to ease concerns about its integrity that might be aroused if it were known that its author was connected to the East India Company, whose monopoly was defended in the tract (Child 1690: 80–90). The publisher dissembled further, claiming that the manuscript accidentally came to his hands after the London fire of 1666, and that the author was 'no Trader' (Child 1690: The Publisher to the Reader). When the text was reprinted several years later with Child's name on the front, the way was open for critics to descry that the public interest would always yield to the private in matters of counsel (Letwin 1963: 39–41).

The general suspicion of merchants was most forcefully expressed by Adam Smith when he wrote that all legislative proposals that came from this order of society needed to be viewed with precaution, for merchants 'have generally an interest to deceive and even to oppress the publick' (Smith 1981 [1776]: Vol. I: 267). The preponderance of merchants in the ranks of counsellors on trade made it more susceptible to charges of self-interest than other genres, as did the corresponding deficit of gentlemen counsellors. One of the proximate causes for this second fact, as Joshua Gee explained, was the influence of the notion that it was below the character of a gentleman to become a merchant, coupled with the related nature of a gentleman's education (Gee 1729: Preface). In a sense, then, we can see counsel on trade as having been parasitic on the prestige of the humanist counsellor, since trade and commerce did not feature in his curriculum. Put differently, the very idea of counsel on trade seemed to tarnish counsel and ask rather a lot of the trader. By the middle of the eighteenth century this tension had begun to ease, partly because books proposing to counsel on the general nature of trade had become an established genre and were being written increasingly by men from the professions (Letwin 1963: 220; Groenewegen 2002: 61–2).

Such a general treatise on trade was attempted by Philip Cantillon, who sought to 'convey a general Idea of Trade' to 'Gentlemen of Power' by 'tracing it to its original Source, and stripping it of that Mystery' it had been covered with, a service that might make it possible for lawmakers to address 'the Abuses crept into the Commerce of this Country' (Cantillon 1759: xvi). A more telling example of the general treatise was Josiah Tucker's commission to write a work on commerce for the Prince of Wales, later George III. The work seems to have been started in 1752, and a portion of the larger projected work was privately circulated in 1755 (Schuyler 1931: 11–12), which was by itself over 170 pages. By contrast, Cavendish's remarks on trade to the future king, just less than 100 years before Tucker's, amounted to only a handful of pages.

It is clear, though, that writings on specific issues still represented the majority of counsel on trade, and this explains something of Joseph Massie's complaint that most commercial writers had 'mixed *personal* with *national* Affairs, and blended *Principles*, *History*, and *Practice* together' (Massie 1760: Dedication). The preponderance of issue-specific pamphlets also explains why peaks in the output of titles seem to be correlated with major controversies, such as the South Sea Bubble of 1720 (Hoppit 2006: 86).

The general treatise was therefore the category in which we can place Smith's *Wealth of Nations*; as Smith made clear, it was intended to serve the statesman's needs when managing the nation's commerce:

> POLITICAL œconomy, considered as a branch of the science of a statesman or legislator, proposes two distinct objects; first, to provide a plentiful revenue or subsistence for the people, or more properly to enable them to provide such a revenue or subsistence for themselves; and secondly, to supply the state or commonwealth with a revenue sufficient for the publick services. It proposes to enrich both the people and the sovereign.
>
> (Smith 1981 [1776]: 428)

The arguments that Smith used to support his counsel were novel, and they had profoundly dislocating effects for the genre he was counselling in, but it is still the statesman that Smith was addressing. Smith's statesman was an ideal type who was schooled in the general principles of trade by the specialist counsellor on trade, the political œconomist. The politics and prejudices of other people are openly acknowledged as inhibiting the statesman from taking all the legislative actions that may be desirable so that Smith's statesman and his counsellor need to be pragmatists (Winch 1983: 501–11).

A few years before Smith, the statesman was portrayed in strongly patriarchal tones by Sir James Steuart: '[w]hat oeconomy is in a family, political oeconomy is in a state' (Steuart 1767: Vol. I: 2).[4] To appreciate this analogy, we need to remember the role of the patriarchal ideal as a projection of good order. For example, in *An Essay on the Happiness and Advantages of a Well-ordered Family*, the following question was asked: 'what hope of *a National Reformation*, if it begin not in *Families*?' The essential assumption at work here was that 'government of these lesser societies' was a precondition for effective rule by magistrates and ministers (Anonymous 1794: 1). Lord North similarly wrote that the family was capable of 'government', and defined œconomy as 'the Art of well governing a mans [*sic*] private house and fortunes', and added that there was no 'necessary Object of *Oeconomy*, save an Owner with his house and possessions'. By this last comment we can take Lord North to have meant that the tasks of œconomy were numerous and diverse, and note that he covered more than 80 topics in his œconomy manual (North 1669: 3). The tasks Steuart required of the good statesman were similarly detailed and thus, unlike Smith's restrained statesman, Steuart's royal patriarch was continuously involved in intricate actions to order the commerce of the polity (Schumpeter 1954a: 176).

This active statesman was still reliant on good counsel if his management was to be effective: '[w]hen principles are well understood, the real consequences of burdensome institutions are clearly seen ... the abuse of the statesman's administration appears palpable' (Steuart 1767: Vol. I: 4). Steuart's comment points us in the direction of an important theme in the counsel given to statesmen by political œconomists that became pronounced in the second half of the eighteenth century: in short, if the statesman intervened ignorantly in the workings of trade, then he was likely to do more harm than good and, in fact, the nature of trade presented limits to the range of feasible actions that the statesman could consider.[5]

The desire to limit the statesman's actions was perhaps most clearly seen in Dugald Stewart's claim that the aim of his science was to 'enlighten those who are destined for the functions of government, and to enlighten public opinion with respect to their conduct'. While Stewart's statesmen and public were routine addressees for counsel, he explicitly set the limits of his science beyond those observed by authors such as James Steuart and Adam Smith – beyond '*Wealth and Population*' or '*the resources of a State*', to encompass the 'happiness and improvement of Political Society' (Stewart 1854–60: Vol. VIII: 9–10, 17).

The scope of Stewart's expanded science is accordingly policy and legislation in general: 'every regulation which affects the sum of national improvement and enjoyment', and his programme was based on a knowledge of the human condition and the motives underlying human action. From here one of the science's central problems came into view, to ascertain 'how far the legitimate province of the Statesman extends'. Once the proper extent of the law was known, it would be possible to demarcate those subjects that belonged to 'the science of Legislation' and those that could be regulated by 'the selfish passions and motives' inherent in human nature (ibid.: Vol. VIII: 16–17). The pretension of Stewart's science was thus not only to advise the statesman as to the good framing of laws, but to define those areas where laws should be made at all.

Jeremy Bentham's conception of political economy was closer to Smith's than to Stewart's, and it was correspondingly narrower in scope. It was first and foremost an art, and one 'exercisible [*sic*] by those who have the government of a nation in their hands', it was 'the art of directing the national industry' (Bentham 1952 [1793–95]: 223). Smith's *Wealth of Nations* was criticized in this context for focusing on science, instead of the art that derives from science, and this deficiency was what Bentham intended his work to redress. On the other hand, Bentham elsewhere divided the field of legislation into four component parts – subsistence, security, abundance, equality – and then distinguished between them based on the level of attention they required from the legislator. Security, for example, made heavy demands on the legislator whereas subsistence did not (Bentham 1954 [1801–4]: 307, 311–12). This variegated terrain of activity for the statesman differed from the continuous field of general legislation described by Stewart.

The point to take from this discussion of the different ways the statesman was imagined and addressed is that the practice and notion of public counsel continued into the eighteenth century largely intact. It was, however, strained by the idea that the nature of trade itself might present limits to the exercise of legislative action upon it. That is, we might see counsel as becoming something other than counsel when it began to assert that the statesman needed not only to modify his actions with reference to counsel but to even refrain from acting altogether. Recalling Hobbes's distinction between command and counsel, it appears that, by the turn of the nineteenth century, counsel was shaping itself as a kind of command, not one couched in the language of sovereignty and obedience but in terms of knowledge and science.

This leads us to consider the shifting relationship between counsellor and statesman in terms of a transition from public counsel to public science (Hutchison 1964: 134–6). Public counsel, even when it insisted on the intractability of certain phenomena to legislation, was still addressed to a statesman or legislator and understood itself as advising this figure regarding good laws. We encounter a different understanding of political economy at the end of the period studied in this book, and it was on display in Nassau Senior's *An Outline of the Science of Political Economy* (Senior 1951 [1836]).

Unlike those presentations that fused together legislative action and the science of trade, Senior distinguished between the 'Science of Political Economy' and the 'Science of legislation'. Legislation was said to require the principles of political economy, but it differed 'in its subject, its premises, and its conclusions'. In brief, legislation was concerned with human welfare at large, whereas political economy was concerned with only one branch – the production and distribution of wealth. Senior's nesting of the science of political economy within a larger framework of knowledge had important implications for the link between his science and the work of legislation, for while the conclusions of political economy regarding wealth may have been 'universally true', they nevertheless did not authorize the political economist to offer even 'a single syllable of advice'. That activity belonged to the writer or statesman who had a view of the larger framework, the science of legislation, and who had weighed all the elements of welfare, not just wealth (ibid.: 2–3).

What we can detect in Senior is the attempt to uncouple political economy from the task of advising the statesman – even the task of advising the statesman not to act – in order to set the science on its own autonomous course. The science itself no longer elaborated the nexus between knowledge and counsel but handed this task onto another agent, the writer or statesman who was concerned with the overarching architecture of government and knowledge. We need to bear in mind, however, that Senior's vision for political economy as an independent science was elaborated in a treatise, and such general works were easily outnumbered by the pamphlet literature that dealt with specific laws and problems. In this shorter litera-ture we can observe the practical maintenance of a link between political economy and counsel, because the publication of pamphlets was often timed to coincide with debates in Parliament over public issues, such as the Bullion Controversy and the Corn Laws (Tribe 1978: 116). It is in relation to the former debate that David Ricardo made his first contribution to political economy, and it was also in connection with this debate that political economy was pilloried in Parliament as a chimerical system of little relevance to making good legislation (Fontana 1985: 123–4). Thus, the austere aspirations of some political economists for a science that functioned independently of the requirements of counsel were undermined indirectly by its connections with a pamphleteering culture, and directly chal-lenged by calls for relevance to the legislative tests of the day. Nevertheless, it is fair to treat Senior's programme as indicating that counsel on trade had largely been surpassed by political economy, which had come to stand as a specialized mode of producing knowledge in relation to phenomena such as trade and wealth, and it therefore marks the end point of our survey.

Conclusion

Counsel on trade was a species of advice to the statesman on how to govern the state wisely, and it projected two organizing discursive figures: the counsellor and the statesman. The counsellor was a prestigious figure who rendered a noble ser-vice to the political community. This umbrella label accommodated the counsellor on trade with some discomfort, for his knowledge was not endorsed by antiquity in the same way as, say, politics was, and he often turned out to be a self-serving merchant. Despite this difficulty, counsel on trade flourished in the late seventeenth century and matured into a genre that could support an impressive list of special-ist treatises by the middle of the eighteenth century. The point to underline is that the figure of the counsellor on trade was publicly available for appropriation, and this required little more than the profession of good intentions. By contrast, the authority of today's economist is secured by a specialist training that imparts knowledge and unique intellectual capacities. Thus, by focusing on counsel we have developed a form of resistance against progressive accounts that would lead us to conflate counsel on trade with economics.

In the early decades of the nineteenth century, counsel on trade morphed into political economy and became imbued in a complex play of trends around its role in public and intellectual life. One of these trends was the decline of the image of the statesman as the addressee of written advice on trade, a figure that was essential to the stability of this genre (Tribe 1978: 83). A factor in this decline was the increasing tendency to see trade as stubbornly resistant to the statesman's attempts to direct it to his own purposes; another was the ambition to fashion political economy into a science concerned with wealth alone, independent of other concerns. Counsel was contesting and combining with science, while the statesman's position as the polity's organizing principle was being superseded by laws of production and distribution. Taking all this together, it is understandable that the relationship between political economy and legislation became uncertain for both the art's advocates and its detractors.

The majority of the titles discussed in what follows fall comfortably into the genre of counsel on trade, and the period of transition to political economy will only concern us in the final chapters of this book. This process will be examined in terms of the emergence of forms of argument that made it possible to cognize the economy as an object distinct from the state. This focus will lead us to look at the unintended *effects* of arguments as much as how they were conceived by the authors who advanced them.

2　Genres of counsel and the administrative state

In the previous chapter we encountered the practice of addressing written counsel to statesmen and a counselling public. Both counsellor and statesman were discursive figures that could be mapped onto English society in diverse ways, from historical figures who literally served as counsellors and statesmen, to merchants who took advantage of the prestige attached to the notion of publicly spirited counsel to advance their private interests. In this chapter, we turn from the idea of counsel in general to specific genres of counsel.

Counsel to government presupposed the state as an entity in its own right. Quentin Skinner has traced the process through which the state came to be understood in this way, as an abstract entity independent from both the rulers who held office and the population who were ruled over. Skinner identified Hobbes as one of the first thinkers to employ this meaning of the state with complete self-confidence, and he suggested that we might therefore construe Hobbes's use of the term as 'marking the end of one phase in the history of political theory' – the phase of thinking of public power in personal terms (Skinner 2002: Vol. II, 368).[1] Skinner's account related to the concept of the sovereign state, that is, the state understood as the locus of political power. Our interest runs parallel to Skinner's because we are also concerned with the state as a presupposition of intellectual argument, but we focus less on how the state was seen as the site of legitimate public power than on how the state was perceived as the site and object of administration.

The essential feature of the administrative state to be underlined is that it was thought to be a complex entity and therefore in need of informed government in multiple domains. In sympathy with Skinner's account, we can note that this idea of the administrative state was also stated with confident clarity by Hobbes. Turning again to Chapter 25 of *Leviathan*, 'Of Counsell', counsel was necessary because 'no man is presumed to have experience in all those things that to the Administration of a great Common-wealth are necessary to be known' (Hobbes 1991 [1651]: 180). These areas included the nature of man, the rights of government, equity, law, justice, honour, strength, the strength of neighbours and enemies. This is a list of domains that required the statesman's attention and, by implication, a list of the topics on which he would require counsel, because administration had come to be understood as exceeding the person of the ruler in terms of both expertise and its points of application.

This is a crucial element of the intellectual context in which we should view the three genres of counsel to be surveyed in what follows. The constitutive purpose of each genre was to assist in the management of some aspect of the state. In our first genre, the analysis of interest, the state was understood to possess interests, in particular, security, trade, and religion; taken together, these interests provided a checklist against which state policy could be assessed and the actions of other states predicted. This genre was therefore a form of meta-counsel, because it could both rank and relate state interests, such as trade and security, but it was most powerfully used to counsel on foreign affairs. The neighbouring genre of political arithmetic provided numerical inventories of states to facilitate policy calculation, and its most important function was to enumerate the sources of a particular state's strength. Counsel on trade provided guidance as to the nature and management of trade, which fed into strength, wealth, and foreign affairs.

We shall see that these genres interacted with each other on the basis of their shared presupposition of the state as both the agent and object of administration. This exercise will enable us to better appreciate the forms of argument that characterized counsel on trade, which we will study in future chapters, and to see how thoroughly arguments regarding trade were tethered analytically to state administration. This last claim about the nexus between trade and state management is central to the overall argument of the book, for in our discussion of Smith and Ricardo we will describe the argumentative mutations these authors introduced into counsel on trade, mutations that abstracted trade into its own domain (the economy) and fashioned a specialized science for it (political economy).

The analysis of interest

In seventeenth-century England, the Italian *ragion di stato* literature provided one model for applying the notion of interest to political affairs (Gunn 1969: 36; Tuck 1993: Chapter 2). Giovanni Botero, for example, castigated Machiavelli in his *Della Ragion di Stato* of 1589 because Machiavelli 'bases his Reason of State on lack of conscience', while Botero wanted to harmonize reason of state with the law of God.[2] Botero nevertheless maintained that it 'should be taken for granted that in the decisions made by princes interest will always override every other argument' (Botero 1956 [1589]: xiii–xiv, 41). By the early seventeenth century, the terms 'reason of state' and 'interest' enjoyed wide currency in western Europe, not least because they opened up matters of state to public scrutiny (Malcolm 2007: 93).

Making statecraft publicly calculable was exactly what the analysis of interest genre purported to do. Its propagation in England was due to Duke Henri de Rohan's pioneering text, *The Interest of Princes*, a work intended to aid Cardinal Richelieu in forming French external policy. Its English preface proclaimed that it was possible to predict the behaviour of states: 'The PRINCES *command* the People, & the Interest *commands the* Princes.' Rohan portrayed Europe as dominated by two powers, the '*Houses of* France *and* Spaine', while all other rulers shifted their alliances as served their own interests (Rohan 1641: Part I, Preface). English translations of Rohan's text were quickly printed and during the Civil War the broader language of interest was found to be amenable to Royalist and republican purposes alike (Gunn 1968: 553–4; Gunn 1969: 35–54). Royalists asserted that private and public interests were united only in the person of the monarch (Houston 1991: 80–1), while republicans claimed to demonstrate the necessary incompatibility between monarchy as a form of government and the end of realizing the common interest (Scott 1988: 208–9). Despite these conflicting uses, during the second half of the seventeenth century the analysis of interest stabilized along the lines of Rohan's text and produced 'the genre of "interest of England" works' (Gunn 1969: 3).

The starting point for this genre was to characterize a state in terms of its key interests, typically security, trade, and religion. England's special situation as an island determined its security interest, as the country could not be invaded easily nor could it feasibly maintain a land empire on the continent. One of the most prolific interest pamphleteers, Slingsby Bethel, thus prescribed England's role in foreign affairs as 'weighing the Imperial powers of Christendome, keeping the ballance, by adding to, or diminishing from any of them' (Bethel 1671: 28). Maintaining the balance of power had become a 'Fundamentall Maxim in the Government of *England*', most especially in relation to the rivalry between Spain and France, and in doing so England served the common interest of Europe (Hill 1673: Section XI).

A state's trade interest was closely related to its security interest. As we will see in the next chapter, trade was thought to be the essential source of state power; it was the '*vena porta* of the Kingdom, and without which the Limbs and Members thereof must be feeble and weak' (de Britaine 1672: 11–12). It follows that trade patterns and the balance of power implied one another; hence, a losing trade with one's allies was not nearly as dangerous as a losing trade with one's enemies. This reasoning led an agitated Bethel to write that 'the *French* set up for an *Universal Commerce* as well as for an *Universal Monarchy*. And in effect, the One is but a necessary consequent upon the other' (Bethel 1677: 11).

In the context of the Third Anglo-Dutch War (1672–74), when the faith of Charles II was in doubt, and in a century when confessional conflict was endemic, religion was treated as a crucial state interest. During the war, counsellors urged that the reformed faith be 'the Polar Star' by which the ship of state was steered (Hill 1673: Section II). Yet we should note that as the Anglo-Dutch state building that followed the Glorious Revolution secured the future of Protestantism (Brewer 1990; Scott 2000), the status of religion as a national interest declined in this genre of counsel. Indeed, even in the seventeenth century, religion regularly featured below security and trade in rankings of state interests. One anonymous author writing in the second half of the eighteenth century described England's confederacy with the Dutch as arising from the common threat posed by France, a union further cemented by 'some resemblance of religion, as opposed to popery'. Ultimately, however, any 'alliance between them will last no longer than their common safety or common profit is endangered' (Anonymous 1759: 215). The interests of religion and security could be variously entwined, or not at all.[3]

After identifying a state's interests, the second essential move of the analysis was to identify when a state was behaving inconsistently with its true interests, and to explain the causes of this divergence, which were reduced to two: because the rulers of a state misjudged its true interests; and because the rulers of a state pursued their own private interests at the expense of the state.

Interests could be misjudged because they changed over time, in correspondence with changes in a nation's manners and government, as when a monarchical government became republican, or because of shifts in the balance of power. Thus it was possible for a state to pursue interests that were no longer appropriate for the conditions of Europe. A favourite example in this context was the persistence of the belief that Spain represented the greatest threat to peace even after France had clearly eclipsed her in power and ambition. Maxims of this type were like '*the Stars to Navigators, rightly understood, the best Guide, and mistaken, the most dangerous*' (Bethel 1671: Preface).

We find a complementary idea in *Letters on the Study and Use of History*, a transposition of the analysis of interest into classical history by Henry St. John, Viscount Bolingbroke. Bolingbroke reflected on his years in the state's service for the benefit of future statesmen,[4] and he described how change in world politics was not only a matter of great events, such as the destruction of some governments and the rise of others, but was also wrought within peoples and governments gradually and 'almost imperceptibly'. Such changes could redound on and accumulate between states, thereby giving rise to epochal shifts that engender 'new interests', which in turn 'beget new maxims of government' (Bolingbroke 1970 [1752]: Vol. I: 199–200). A further complication was that 'the balance of power would never be exactly poised', and neither was it possible to discern the exact point of equality (ibid.: Vol. II: 47).

In addition to these intrinsic difficulties, interests were also mistaken due to the ruler's poor or insufficient reasoning. One author argued in this vein that England warred with the Dutch for 'imaginary Advantages', such as the assumption that England would gain the Dutch trade after their destruction (Du Moulin 1673: 30). The cause most commonly offered for statesmen's poor reasoning was their impairment by passion or animosity, something to which kings were said to be highly susceptible (McWard 1672: 4). In sum, nothing was 'more ordinary in the world then *gross mistakes* in the *Interest* of Countries' (Bethel 1673: 10).

The reasoning of statesmen could be portrayed as deficient because the state was seen as an entity independent of the office of king or sovereign; this understanding of the state was reinforced by the other line of analysis that purported to explain why a state might be directed away from its true interests – because its rulers pursued their own private interests. In relation to the rise of France as Europe's dominant power, Bolingbroke wrote that either Cromwell did not discern this turn of affairs, or had followed 'private interest to act against the general interest of Europe' (Bolingbroke 1970 [1752]: Vol. I: 258). More desperately, Charles II joined with the French against the Dutch in the Third Anglo-Dutch War, and this made it possible for France to become the dominant power in Europe. Bolingbroke felt obliged to ascribe this act to Charles II having been 'favourable to the popish interest' (ibid.: Vol. I: 284). In short, the interests of states were not always well perceived, and even when they were, they were not always well pursued.

The final operation that characterized the analysis of interest was connecting state behaviour with the balance of power, an interest the nations of Europe held in common. We regularly find that predictions were made regarding what a certain event would mean for the European balance. This is the purpose that Bolingbroke gave to the study of history: history augmented experience by showing us causes and allowing us to guess at future events (ibid.: Vol. I: 49). For example, Bethel declared that the English and the Dutch were together 'Masters of Naval strength', and that this union was unassailable by any combination of European powers. The French could therefore never achieve universal monarchy while the two maritime powers maintained a 'true intelligence', since together they could always reduce France at sea and therefore in commerce, causing its land power to wither in consequence. If, however, France were to gain the ports and provinces of the Netherlands, it would attain the strength and position needed to achieve universal monarchy (Bethel 1671: 27–31). In a different tract, Bethel made an identical prediction, only this time conditional on the French establishing a strategic position in the Northern Seas (Bethel 1673: 11). More sophisticated scenarios were also developed in this genre, such as the consequences of the Netherlands falling under French control. One author explored the implications of this event for different nations in terms of trade patterns, taxes, and the supply of men. Thus the relevant maxim was 'it is not enough to consider power absolutely, but allso the management thereof' (Hill 1673: Section VII).

The genre acquired an added element of predictive power when forecasts of balance of power dynamics were combined with a knowledge of the particular characteristics of a nation, often referred to as its 'situation'. The Dutch were seen to be compelled by their trade interest to maintain an alliance with Denmark, Persia, and the Turks, who served as markets for their commodities; the limited agricultural capacity of the Dutch likewise obliged them to keep a close friendship with Poland for its corn exports (Aglionby 1671: 127–30). The French, by contrast, were given to be warlike because of the extent of their territories, the fruitfulness of their soil, prodigious revenues, unchecked form of rule, and the weakness of their neighbours. France's only vulnerability was naval strength, and so this became a prime interest of France and made its actions predictable (Du Moulin 1673: 3, 6–7). Such is the geo-political strategizing that the analysis of interest was used to provide.

Having sketched the analysis of interest, we can now offer a summary. It was a species of political knowledge, in the sense that it treated states as '*objects for rational and considering men*' (Aglionby 1671: Preface), or as entities that could be studied in their own right by methods available to learned persons. The genre therefore made the state and state policy both visible and calculable, and it duly became an established genre for those wishing to guide statesmen, to defend them, or to suggest the folly of their actions in relation to the interests of the states they governed. All of these uses presupposed the state as a real entity with interests in its own right, as a state, which were shaped by particular circumstances. Actions inconsistent with this explanatory apparatus were understood as the consequences of false or corrupt motivations on the part of statesmen. The analysis of interest was therefore descriptive, prescriptive, and predictive. In the words of Bethel: 'it is certain, that all *Nations* will increase, or decline more or less, according as their *Interest* is pursued' (Bethel 1673: 8).

Political arithmetic

In an essay that popularized mathematical learning, John Arbuthnot urged the keeping of public accounts that would 'regard the whole State of a Common-wealth'. The accounts should pertain to the number of people, balance of trade, public revenues, and military power by sea and land. He claimed that this was the 'true *Political* Knowledge', whose usefulness had been proved by William Petty and others writing on the subject of political arithmetic (Arbuthnot 1745: 19–20). This was the name commonly given to calculations of this type. In Richard Rolt's *A New Dictionary of Trade and Commerce*, political arithmetic was defined as 'the application of arithmetical calculations to political uses and subjects, [such] as the public revenues, number of people ... or whatever relates to the power, strength, riches, &c. of any nation' (Rolt 1756: s.v. 'political arithmetic'). Another name for political arithmetic was 'statistics':

> STATISTICS are that comprehensive Part of municipal Philosophy, which states and defines the Situation, Strength, and Resources of a Nation, and is a Kind of political Abstract, by which the Statesman may be enabled to calculate his Finances, as well as guide the Œconomy of his Government.
>
> (Capper 1801: vii)

If one recalls the difficulties involved in assessing the relative strengths of rival states and the fundamental importance of these data for the balance of power, the utility of political arithmetic as a calculating aid for statesmen becomes evident, as it reduced balance of power assessments to an arithmetical operation. This is how Charles Davenant portrayed its role in his *Discourses on the Public Revenues*. Davenant acknowledged the foundational contribution of Petty, but claimed that Petty had over-estimated the strength of England and under-estimated the strength of other states. One of the proximate causes of Petty's errors was that the increasing power of France stood as a 'very unpleasant Object for the Parliament' that 'did disquiet the Mind of King *Charles* II'. The fact that Petty's calculations suggested a minimal disparity in power between France and England justified the actions of Charles II, who breached the Triple Alliance with the Dutch and joined with France, an act that was 'pernicious to the Interest of *England*'. This led Davenant to suggest that, on the issue of the strength of France, Petty 'rather made his Court, than spoke his Mind' (Davenant 1698: Vol. I: 3–6).

According to Davenant, the wise statesman would not prefer a political seda-tive over bracing counsel. Instead, he and his counsellors would use political arithmetic to 'Compute and Compare the Power and Riches of the Adverse Party', including which state could endure a war for longer and how that endurance might be increased. The costs of war to the state were like bleeding to the body, and while a state might indefinitely bear 'moderate Bleedings' (say, three million a year), it could die at the loss of great quantities of blood (say, twenty million in three or four years). At the same time, statesmen also needed to know the strength of their allies to ensure that these states made honourable contributions to the war effort (ibid.: Vol. I: 7–9). Davenant's friend and source of estimates, Gregory King, calculated that each year from 1688 to 1695 England had decreased by three million sterling, while France decreased by six million, and that the overall ratio of decline between the two states was 6:7 in England's favour, while Holland enjoyed a modest increase over the same period of time (King 1973 [1696]: 69). Political arithmetic was therefore a way of computing relative strengths to guard against misjudging a state's balance of power interest: 'He that has such a computing Head, will seldom enter into ill Measures' (Davenant 1698: Vol. I: 14).

Managing a state's trade in relation to the balance of power was also aided by the computations of political arithmetic. Given the complex nature of the connections between various trades, it was difficult to know which trades were helpful and which hurtful to the public. The temptation was to descry one particular trade without a view of its place in the overall trade of a territory, something like objecting against 'the Motion of one Wheel, without knowing and seeing how the whole Engine moves' (ibid.: Vol. I: 30–1). The desire to accurately assess the effect of specific trades on public welfare informed many of the proposals for a governmental body to oversee the nation's trade. A Council of Trade, for example, was established by a 1650 Act of Parliament. Along with other tasks, it was instructed to 'consider of some way, that an exact account be kept of all commodities imported and exported'. Such an account was to enable a balance of trade to be calculated, and this, in turn, would ensure that the commonwealth was not impoverished by 'receiving commodities yearly from Forraign Parts, of greater value than was carried out' (Anonymous 1657: 408).

Near the turn of the century, Davenant proposed the creation of another Council of Trade to perform a similar task, since if the balance 'were known, Stated and well understood We might thereunto fit and Adapt Sumptuary Lawes, Such as might prohibit at home the Use of Commodities from those Country's [*sic*] where We Loose in the Balance, and where Trade is hurtful to us' (Davenant 1942 [1695]: 53).

Indeed, Davenant authored two reports on the nature of the trade between Britain and various nations, with regard to the primary goods traded, their values, and who the balance of trade with each nation favoured. And he suggested that the particulars he presented enabled England's interests to be protected from states that sought to 'enlarge themselves at our Expense' (Davenant 1715: Part II: 65).

The prime target that Davenant had in sight here was the Dutch, England's 'most dangerous Rivals in Trade', who required 'a watchful Eye over all their Proceedings' in trade (ibid.: Part II: 72). The appropriate response was not in the order of 'an open Breach', but 'strong and steady Councils', or good policy. More interesting was his reason why this was the appropriate form of competition with the Dutch: 'the Common-Concerns of Religion, which should always link together *Great Britain* and the *United Provinces*' (ibid.: Part II: 67–9). In contradistinction, England's warring with France was a response to her use of prohibitions to gain mastery over England's trade and thereby her strength too, a situation that their religious interests did not neutralize but inflame. War, then, was the appropriate response to France because it pursued universal monarchy. Davenant predicted that at the eventual end of the war, 'their mutual Interest would incline 'em to listen to Terms of a fair commercial Treaty'. For Davenant, such a situation was acceptable to England in terms of its effects on France's strength, primarily due to England's natural advantages in certain manufactures, which ensured that 'a Free Trade with *France* can never be Dangerous' to England (ibid.: Part I: 57–8, 60).[5]

Political arithmetic was also proffered as an aid to the state's internal administration due to its ability to render the anatomy of the state visible and therefore susceptible to direct management. A clear instance of this was John Graunt's answer to his own question: why was this numerical knowledge of the state important? He claimed that the 'Art of Governing' was to secure peace and plenty, and to provide 'good, certain, and easie Government'. Information was essential to carry out this task effectively, that is, to 'understand the Land, and the hands of the Territory to be governed'. His examples of good government included knowing in what regions there were sufficient numbers to support establishing a trade, and knowing the different employments of the people, especially those that were superfluous to the state's needs (Graunt 1973 [1662]: 72–4). Government needed to be able to act on the territory: to establish trade, to press men, and to levy taxes; for these tasks to be carried on effectively, the territory needed to be rendered knowable in these same terms.

In his *Political Arithmetick*, William Petty segmented the population in a broader fashion than Graunt had done, claiming that all nations were largely composed of a few key groups: husbandmen, seamen, soldiers, artisans, and merchants. The seaman was to be prized above the rest because he had the skills of soldier, merchant, and seaman, in effect he was 'three Husbandmen' (Petty 1690: 18). In a similar vein, Arthur Young argued that a detailed knowledge of the population would yield several advantages to a state's administration. Reminiscent of Graunt, even though he was writing more than a century later, Young insisted on the utility the state would derive from knowing both the location of 'supernumeraries' who could be conscripted into armies and navies without harming the nation's trade, and where to find the pockets of wealth necessary to support these forces once they had been raised (Young 1771: 7–9, 12, 17). In these examples we see how the manner of the territory's anatomization was conditioned by the concern with state strength. In this light, consider William Mildmay's claim that a good administration would 'REGULATE the various employment of the people' because it was the people's 'good order, like the discipline of an army, that procures strength and power to a kingdom' (Mildmay 1765: 10).

The calculations central to political arithmetic appear spurious to contemporary readers. Petty, for example, calculated that the average person's expense was £7 per annum, and if England had a population of 10 million, then a mere tax of 10 per cent of the per capita annual expense would provide enough revenue to provide for a navy of 40,000, plus an army of 100,000 foot soldiers (Petty 1690: 102). It was with calculations of this kind, using 'Terms of *Number*, *Weight*, or *Measure*' (ibid.: Preface), that Petty wanted to set the knowledge of the state on surer ground. Even more startling to today's reader is Gregory King's calculations of the peopling of the world after the Flood by eight persons (King 1973 [1696]: 41). From today's perspective, it is hard to recognize the empirical content of this literature,[6] and complaints about this aspect of political arithmetic ghosted the genre from its beginning. This is the perspective in which to see not only Adam Smith's doubts over the value of political arithmetic (Smith 1981 [1776]: Vol. I: 534–5), but remedial proposals such as Arthur Young's programme to enumerate the people every five years. Young claimed that without a supporting scheme of this type, political arithmetic would continue to operate with 'such imperfect authority, and with such great variations, that no sure dependance is to be placed in such random ideas'. The consequences of working with 'mere *guesses*' was that the 'Administration is as ignorant of the point as other people: the ministers of state have no better opportunities of *accurate* information in this very important affair, than the lowest clerk in office' (Young 1771: 4–6).

While Young's concerns were no doubt valid, ability and ambition are different things, and the ambition inherent in political arithmetic was to make the state's strength calculable and administrable. Thus, this genre is also a political knowledge – a knowledge of the state – and it intersected with other state knowledges such as the analysis of interest and counsel on trade. One crucial intersection was the ability of political arithmetic to ameliorate errors when calculating state interests through its purported computing power, in particular the balance of power. Another locus was the management of state interests, such as trade, which could be better nursed by statesmen once they were armed with a numerical knowledge of their territory, a knowledge that political arithmeticians would supply. In the following and final section of this chapter we focus on these intersections in a classic text from the beginning of our period of counsel on trade, Thomas Mun's *England's Treasure by Forraign Trade*.

Counsel on trade

Nicholas Barbon wrote that Livy, like other ancient writers, took no notice of trade, and that this was true even of a comparatively modern writer like Machiavelli, who '*doth not mention* Trade, *as any way interested in the Affairs of State*' (Barbon 1690: Preface). David Hume also noted the general silence of the ancients on this topic, and suggested that 'Trade was never esteemed an affair of state till the last century'; this testified to an advance in government dating from modern times, alongside the widespread understanding of the balance of power system and the improved 'internal POLICE' of states (Hume 1985 [1777]: 88, 93).[7] Thomas Mun also presented trade as an affair of state in *England's Treasure by Forraign Trade*. In his prefatory address, Mun described money as an object of 'Policy', essential to both the preservation and enlargement of the commonwealth. He concluded his work by invoking a 'Principal in Reason of State', that whatever supports the commonwealth should be nursed and protected, in this case, foreign trade (Mun 1928 [1664]: viii, 88).

Mun's tract had a pleasing unity that stemmed from his central contention: if a kingdom was to grow in wealth and treasure, it must 'sell more to strangers yearly than wee consume of theirs in value'. The difference in the value of wares must by necessity be returned to the kingdom in treasure. The relevant analogy was with the estate of a private man who had an annual revenue of £1000 but lived on only £500, and thus his estate grew by the remaining £500 each year (ibid.: 5). Mun then intervened into diverse topics of debate on the basis of this maxim. He confidently denied the popularly held opinion that exporting money harmed the kingdom. If bullion was exported in exchange for goods that were then sold at a profit, then the nation's balance would be favourably improved, which, as he claimed to have already demonstrated, ultimately governed the flow of treasure (ibid.: 16).

A kingdom should concern itself with treasure because it represented the sinews of war: it 'doth provide, unite & move the power of men, victuals, and munition' (ibid.: 70). At times Mun pursued this guiding aim along two parallel tracks, one relating to the prince's wealth and one relating to the kingdom's wealth, and in these moments we also see his advice divided between, on the one hand, the Machiavellian concern with how the prince might maintain his *stato* and, on the other, how the kingdom could be made powerful. In short, there is a tension here between conceiving power in personal terms and conceiving power in abstract terms – from the perspective of the state as an impersonal institution.

An indicative instance of this tension related to treasure and the prince's safety. Mun argued against the opinion that princes were corrupted by storing bullion and instead asserted that it was necessary to have a sum at ready command (although wise rulers would dissociate themselves from unpopular taxes by having them levied by Parliament) (ibid.: 65–7). The prince was further advised to measure the amount of treasure he stored each year not by the surplus of his revenues over his costs, but by the balance of trade, lest he impoverish the polity. In fact, a wise prince would not simply store treasure but return it to his subjects in useful ways, by having ships of war built and by creating stores of armaments and munitions. The prince was 'like the stomach in the body, which if it cease to digest and distribute to the other members, it doth no sooner corrupt them, but it destroyes it self' (ibid.: 70). Thus, the tension between prince and kingdom was resolved via the circulation metaphor, which located the prince as only one of the state's elements, which must be subjected to the functional requirements of the whole.

The territory was the object of Mun's recommendations on how to increase exports and decrease imports, thereby improving the balance of trade. In the several programmes that Mun elaborated for this end, the state's population was construed in terms of large groups of the type we have already encountered in political arithmetic, such as the poor, who seemingly existed as a resource that could be deployed to various uses. For example, the poor were to be set to producing luxury clothing to extinguish the need for its importation, and to fishing, which would transform them into mariners and encourage shipping (ibid.: 8–9, 11). The other overlap to notice between counsel on trade and political arithmetic was Mun's proposal for the state's balance of foreign trade to be officially calculated, a procedure which should be carried on by His Majesty's customs officers to allow 'the State to discover how we prosper or decline in this great and weighty business' (ibid.: 83). This scheme was a switch point between the two genres, which allows us to observe how counsel on trade and political arithmetic could be articulated: in this case, a programme designed to augment the state's wealth was to be coupled with an enumerative technology to guide its operation.

If we turn now to inter-state rivalry, we see that Mun's analysis was developed through a comparison of the two sources of wealth, natural (from the land and sea) and artificial (from manufacturing and trading), which was then doubled by a comparison between England and the Netherlands. England was rich in natural wealth, large, well provisioned, and ably situated for defence. But all this fortune had made the people lazy, luxurious, and weak. The Hollanders' territory, by contrast, was small and lacked natural wealth, which had forced its people to grow wise and industrious. The chief point of application for these virtues, and the base of Dutch strength and wealth, was the fishing they carried on in English seas. This crucial trade supported Dutch shipping, royal revenues, and the population's subsistence. Mun's counsel turned on the fact that the right to fish in these seas was a matter of swords and not words (ibid.: 71–5). He advised that while the Dutch were in league with England and at war with Spain, it would be England's good policy to permit the Dutch access to this source of strength. If, however, the Dutch were to be subjected to Spanish rule, then England's good policy would clearly be reversed. In fact, even the belief that the Dutch were England's natural ally stood in need of inspection, for foreign observers were said to wonder that the English only looked fearfully on Spanish and French power. After all, it was the Dutch who most eclipsed England in navigation and trade, and who nursed an ambition for greatness on the world stage (ibid.: 76–82). We can note that Mun's counsel on Anglo-Dutch relations, where trade and friend–enemy assessments were dynamic and mutually conditioning, looked remarkably like the analysis of interest, minus the actual language of interest.[8]

While state security was central to this analysis, it is important to remember the primacy of Mun's balance of trade doctrine in the overall context of his tract. For example, Mun acknowledged the temptation to restrict the export of certain essential goods, such as victuals and munitions, except in exchange for bullion. Such a policy would be unsuccessful, however, because only a favourable balance of trade kept money in a kingdom, and if it was gathered by any other means, the effect would only be temporary: 'whatsoever is forced in one way must out again another way' (ibid.: 37). Just as the prince was seen earlier to be reduced to an element (the stomach) of a broader system of circulation, so too are certain customary recourses to sovereign action presented as ineffectual due to the nature of the process that was to be governed: the balance of trade gave the rule to policy. This point revisits the theme of counsel's setting limits to sovereignty in a way that jeopardized its status as counsel, and we have come close to Foucault's thesis about the displacement of sovereignty by political economy, a topic considered in Chapter 3, which deals with counsel on trade at length.

Conclusion

Counsel on trade thus shared the administrative character of the analysis of interest and political arithmetic, which derived from their common presupposition of what we have been calling the administrative state. The essential idea embodied in this term is that the state was something beyond the person of the ruler and needed to be managed as such – as a complicated entity in its own right.[9] Our three genres focused on aspects of state administration that were called forth by the fact of the state's existence in a threatening world of rival states: the geopolitical situation of the state was the prime concern of the analysis of interest; political arithmetic provided a means for estimating and anatomizing the strength of the state; and counsel on trade was concerned with the sources of state strength and wealth and how they could be nurtured. As these summary descriptions suggest, these genres overlapped with each other in important places. For example, political arithmetic and counsel on trade construed the state's population in terms of certain groups, such as the poor and sailors. These groups were identified to the state not on the basis of the moral identities they were capable of performing, or their place in a scheme of distribution, but with reference to their contribution to state power. Similarly, Mun did not describe Anglo-Dutch relations in the idiom of natural law, but through an improvised analysis of the geo-strategic situation of the English state. Thus, the shared concern with the administration of the state vis-à-vis its power and survival meant that these genres were porous to one another.

Identifying these related genres of counsel and indicating their close relationship via the administrative state in this way is important for two aspects of the account to be developed in forthcoming chapters. First, it provides the perspective from which we will understand how the same author could write in more than one genre, or combine two or more genres in the same tract. While it is possible to provide distinguishing accounts of our three genres with reference to founding authorities, peculiar vocabularies, and so on, our primary concern is with the effects of their forms of argument, that is, the objects that could be cognized by the counsellors who mobilized these forms of argument. As we have seen, for our three genres this object was the state, which needed to manage its place in geopolitics, understand its own strength, and grow in strength and wealth. The second reason why having a sense of the relationship between these genres is important is because it will enable us to detect when the ground of their relationship started to shift. More specifically, so long as counsellors wrote about trade in relation to the needs of the state, they maintained a close correspondence with other state knowledges, such as the analysis of interest and political arithmetic. We will observe in future chapters that Smith and Ricardo developed new forms of argument that related to theoretical objects other than the state – the national economy and the international economy – and this altered the relationship between counsel on trade and its cognate genres of counsel.

Part II
Counsel on trade

3   The state's strength and wealth

We now have a sense of the context in which counsel on trade operated, including the two key intellectual presuppositions that shaped its concerns. The first of these was the propriety of offering written counsel to the figure of the statesman, and the second was the position of the administrative state as the target of these counsels. Attention now turns to the type of actions that were recommended and how they were constructed discursively.

State security was a dominant concern due to the threatening world the state was seen to exist in. The most important evidence of this in counsel on trade is found in the concurrent analysis of state strength and wealth. This meant that wealth did not function as a generic category in arguments about trade in the way we are familiar with today through concepts such as national income and utility. Instead, wealth was subjected to attempts to sequester its valuable parts, such as bullion, and guard against its dangerous components, such as luxury. This concern with strength and wealth was tempered by the fact that trade was analysed as a complex process, and hence it could be portrayed as resistant to state attempts to intervene in it in an instrumental fashion. Yet our key point in this chapter will be that these forms of argument did not make the economy cognizable as an object distinct from the state, and this point will allow us to distinguish counsel on trade from Ricardo's political economy in future chapters. We will begin our characterization with the relationship between strength and wealth, and then turn to consider how this fixation generated tensions within the genre.

Strength and wealth

Nicholas Barbon offered an explanation of why strength and trade had become so closely intertwined in his preface to *A Discourse of Trade*. Following the invention of gun powder, the stones and wooden engines that had been the ammunition and artillery of the Greeks and Romans had fallen out of use and been replaced by lead and cannon. The old weapons were easily procured and fashioned, while the new instruments were made from materials – such as iron and brimstone – that were not found in all countries, in which case they needed to be imported. Hence, 'Trade *is now become as necessary to Preserve Governments, as it is useful to make them Rich*' (Barbon 1690: Preface). In other words, trade provided the very materials that constituted state strength, and it was therefore integral to security.

John Brewer sounded a related note in his invaluable study of the English fiscal-military state (Brewer 1990).[1] The Glorious Revolution of 1688 allowed England to stabilize confessional issues and focus on state-building, in particular by improving the efficiency of taxation, professionalizing the civil service, and developing public debt markets. These institutions represented an administrative prowess that was essential to military victory because they made it possible to extract the amazing quantities of money, men, and supplies necessary to sustain ongoing conflict in Europe and further abroad. No doubt the same point about the staggering costs of war holds today; the difference was both the regularity of war and the *share* of public wealth that the state needed to mobilize. The intensity of the demands of war in the early modern period both created the fiscal-military state and subjected it to regular strains.

One striking illustration of the fiscal needs of the early-modern state is provided by comparing the cost of a multi-storey cotton spinning mill late in the eighteenth century, at £5,000, with the cost of the 1765 first-rate ship *Victory*, at £63,174 (ibid.: 34). Another is Ashley's estimate that in 1657, when Cromwell was attempting to spoil the Spanish bid for universal monarchy, spending on the army was 66 per cent of total revenue, while naval expenditure represented 26 per cent – together taking over 90 per cent of total state spending (Ashley 1934: 48). Despite the drain they represented to a state's resources, seventeenth-century armies were not well provisioned, armed, or trained, and they regularly mutinied for lack of wages. Cardinal Richelieu thought that more armies were ruined by lack of supplies and disarray than by battle (quoted in Kennedy 1988: 91). Such a fate befell the English fleet at Chatham in 1667, during the second Anglo-Dutch War, when the Dutch sailed up the Medway and burned the English ships, which scarce resources had helped to keep laid-up in dock (Jones 1980: 80–1).

Another stress inherent in the fiscal-military state was its need to lay claim to labour, which issued in the potentially violent practice of impressment. It was used in every major eighteenth-century war in which Britain participated to boost the army's numbers, while naval impressment was both more common and unpopular. The natural target for the naval press gang was the British merchant marine, because the Navy did not want to take on untrained men, such as those who were turned out of gaols (Brewer 1990: 49–51). Legal discourse acknowledged the legitimacy of impressment, along with the Navy's reliance on shipowners to train seamen, a dependency that was conveyed in the description of shipping as a 'nursery' for seamen, which we saw Cavendish use in his advice to the Prince of Wales in Chapter 1. This reliance also explains a 1740 Act that was designed to encourage merchant recruiting by prohibiting a landsman from being pressed during his first two years at sea (Baugh 1965: 170–1). The merchant marine, however, was simply not large enough to supply the manpower needs of the Royal Navy. At the height of the Seven Years' War, for example, nearly 90,000 men served in the Navy, while merchant mariners numbered around half that total (Neal 1977: 21–2). Hence, the number of seamen was a point 'upon the Anvil of the State', one 'hard enough for the hammering of all the political Smiths of the Nation' (Defoe 1728a: 365).

In addition to money and men, the war machines of Europe needed ponderous quantities of strategic materials. Naval supplies, for example, needed to be stock-piled and their prices rose once war began (Neal 1977: 30). The fact that some goods were indispensable to military effectiveness introduced a geo-logistical element into European conflict. Here we can note that the Baltic trade was an essential supplier of naval stores until the 1790s (Jones 1980: 23). The Baltic was controlled by Denmark, who joined the Dutch during the first and second Anglo-Dutch Wars, which forced England to accept smaller supplies of lower quality from alternative locations, a development that contributed to the catastrophic decision to leave the fleet in dock at Chatham in 1667 (Jones 1996: 26). Likewise, in 1778, France had placed large timber orders for ship construction and the British, falsely believing that France was seriously afflicted by timber shortages, seized her supply ships in 1779 even though they were being escorted by the neutral Dutch (Dull 1975: 174–6, 208). The active Anglo-Dutch treaty held that naval supplies were not contraband, and hence could be carried legally to Britain's enemies (Scott 1990: 284–5). Thus, the price Britain willingly paid to assert control over the supply of strategic materials was to open hostilities with the Dutch (Mackesy 1964: 377–9).

The fiscal-military state voraciously consumed money, men, and goods, which in turn were targets for various administrative programmes. Our task for the remainder of this chapter is to inquire how the fact of the state's material needs was correlated with counsel on trade. One part of the answer was suggested earlier, when we encountered Thomas Mun's description of money as the sinews of war because it commanded men, victuals, and munition. In other words, it was recognized that trade was an important affair of state because, as Nicholas Barbon implied, it provided the state with the very stuff of strength.

This idea could also be seen in the characterizations of Dutch power that were prevalent in the seventeenth century, when this nation was treated as a model for good policy because it had rapidly risen to the status of world power despite being a small state with limited scope for agriculture. In *The Dutch Drawn to the Life*, which was rather like a seventeenth-century 'guide to the Dutch', the immediate sources of Dutch strength were reduced to four: sea defences; fortifications; their stock and supply of ammunitions; and their disciplined and well paid army. This account was immediately complicated by the claim that the Dutch 'thrive and grow rich by Warre', and this for a slew of reasons including the positive effects of war on their shipping and excise revenues (Anonymous 1664: 42, 50–2). In response to the question of how the Dutch nation could have increased in power and wealth so rapidly, the author offered six reasons: industrious national character, control of the nation's water for defence, access to the Baltic Sea and hence military supplies, use of navigation and trade to replace land as the source of wealth that then yields ships and sailors, access to waterways that facilitated trafficking goods, and providing each major town with its own staple good, such as cloth in Rotterdam, and the Indies trade in Amsterdam (ibid.: 104–8, 112). In a later pamphlet by Joseph Hill, *The Interest of these United Provinces*, we find a similar assessment of Dutch strength along multiple axes, namely, control of water for defence, extensive fortifications, supply of ships and ammunition, the number and quality of Dutch fighting men, and the supply of money and food needed to maintain these men (Hill 1673: Section IX).

What we can see in these enumerations is that the sources of a nation's strength formed a variegated terrain of interrelated elements; strength was not a smooth category. Nevertheless, it is clear enough that the state's ability to supply its war needs – money, men, and militarily useful goods – was thought to be fundamentally important to its security. This was the crucial service that trade was seen to perform, and why it had become an affair of state. Keeping this point in mind allows us to make perfect sense of why counsellors on trade made it a regular practice to comment on the utility of a given policy for state strength.

John Locke and David Hume are telling examples. In standard histories of economic thought, both are regularly nominated as the Fathers of the quantity theory of money. Accordingly, they are credited with the insight that price was a ratio between the quantity of money and the quantity of goods in a nation. The implication, supposedly devastating for 'bullionism', was that gold and silver were not real wealth. Yet both emphasized the link between a ready supply of money and state power. Locke wrote that the value of money in general was 'the quantity of all the Money in the World, in proportion to all the Trade', and the value of money at a national level was governed by the same proportion (Locke 1991 [1696]: Vol. I: 265). But Locke also claimed that if a rival state came to exceed the home state in supply of money, then they 'can maintain a greater force' and 'on any occasion ingross Naval and Warlike Stores, and thereby endanger us' (ibid.: Vol. II: 419).[2] Hume likewise insisted that for any kingdom, 'the greater or less plenty of money is of no consequence; since the prices of commodities are always proportioned to the plenty of money'. It follows that a greater quantity of money will raise prices and thus prejudice trade. Hence, it 'is only the *public* which draws any advantage from the greater plenty of money; and that only in its wars and negociations with foreign states', through its ability to 'have employed mercenary troops, which they hired from their poorer neighbours'. More generally, however, 'men and commodities are the real strength of any community' (Hume 1985 [1777]: 281–2, 293). Hume, the arch quantity theorist, thought about state power in relation to men, money, and goods, just like his contemporaries.

The trade–strength nexus also helps us to understand pamphlets such as Daniel Defoe's (1728b) *Some Considerations on the Reasonableness and Necessity of Encreasing and Encouraging the Seamen*. Defoe's dilemma was how to ensure an adequate supply of seamen for both the Royal Navy and the merchant marine. It was a nice conundrum, since in war time the king must have seamen from the merchant marine or 'the Service is starv'd', while in peace time 'the Merchants must employ them, or they starve'. After the end of the war, the Royal Navy's needs dropped from 'fifty or sixty thousand Seamen' to 'very few', which meant these men were largely lost to the state because they had to take up employment elsewhere, or were drawn into the merchant marine, the service of foreign princes, or piracy (Defoe 1728b: 7–8, 13–14). Defoe's solution involved that most plastic resource of the early modern imagination, the poor, who were to be trained up for service and held in reserve. Thus, instead of relying on trade as a nursery of seamen, which was then hurt by the public's abuse of it, Defoe proposed that the national service 'be its own Nursery' (ibid.: 46).

The provisioning function that trade performed for state power also explains how wealth could often be used synonymously with strength, such that it too acquired an uneven character. Consider, for example, Joseph Harris's (1757) treatment of wealth in *An Essay Upon Money and Coins*. Wealth and riches were said to consist of those things that supplied 'the comfortable subsistence of human life', and they originated from either the land, or the product of land and labour (Harris 1757: 1). In a later section, '*Of the comparative riches or wealth of nations*', Harris immediately slid from the riches and wealth of his section title to 'riches and strength', and stated that they were to be measured not from the extent of dominions or numbers of people, but from a set of factors: the fertility of the soil, the industry and skilfulness of the people, and the quality of their government. Harris then added that riches included the 'stock of those things that are necessary for the support of life, and for defence against enemies'. Once we saw riches in this broad sense, Harris assured us, bullion 'cannot make so considerable a part, as people are apt to imagine' (ibid.: 26–8).

Most authors, however, moved more quickly than Harris when glossing the strength-wealth relation and offered such formulations as 'NATIONAL Power and Wealth consists in Numbers of People, and Magazines of home and Foreign Goods. These depend on Trade, and Trade depends on Money' (Law, 1720: 49); or, 'the *Riches* of a Nation are the *Strength* of it', and what is strength if not 'the *Number of its People*, and its Ability to maintain *Fleets* and *Armies*?' (Webster 1740: 9–10); or, finally, 'the great Source of national Strength is Trade alone, which can at once increase the Treasure and the Numbers of a Nation, which united form the complex Idea of national Strength' (Newton 1756: 13).

Counsellors on trade were thus by definition counsellors on strength. Trade, strength, and wealth came together because they were imbricated in one another and were constituted by the same things. The effect was to license arguments of this form: fishing (trade) produced food (wealth) and sailors (strength); or, equally, employment (fishing) attracted men (strength) and both elements fostered trade (wealth).[3] Substitutions of this type were as variable as they were unremarkable in counsel on trade; the important implication was that trade, strength, and wealth needed to be nurtured together.

As a consequence of these relations, the attempt to foster one element of the state's strength without due sensitivity to its effects on the other elements could be construed as wanting in wisdom. In this regard we can note William Temple's (1758) *A Vindication of Commerce and the Arts*, an irritated defence of commerce against William Bell's attack on it in the name of agriculture. Bell had claimed that population growth was determined by the availability of subsistence, which came from agriculture rather than commerce. Agriculture should therefore form the focus of national policy in order to raise the level of population (Bell 1756). Temple countered that 'people alone are not the strength of a state', and the desire for a large population had to be moderated by the overarching requirement for 'political strength and general safety'. If the kingdom were to become a nation of husbandmen only, whose 'wealth consisted only in corn and cattle', then it would soon become 'a prey to a neighbouring ambitious state', since such a 'system of police' was ill-suited to the reality of Europe, where commerce was needed to produce 'great stocks of money and commodities' (Temple 1758: 1–2, 5).

We are now in a position to offer one part of our answer to the question of how the requirements of the fiscal-military state were connected with counsel on trade. Strength and wealth were seen to consist in the stock and supply of money, men, and militarily useful goods, and trade was a source of them all. Accordingly, the general purpose of counsel on trade was to provide the statesman with the knowledge and practical programmes necessary to increase trade and, with it, the strength and wealth of the state. This leads us to consider how trade as a whole was understood, and the types of programmes that counsellors on trade were prepared to recommend to statesmen for its good management.

Circulation

The most common and important way in which trade was conceived of as a whole was in terms of the circulation of money, men, and goods between parts of the polity. The imagery of circulation was old and rich (see Finkelstein 2000; Huntley 1951; Lowry 1974), and it was mobilized in a number of ways. Anatomy was a powerful analogy in the middle of the seventeenth century. William Petty, for example, endorsed the comparison between '*the* Body Natural, *and* Body Politick*', and asserted that anatomy was the best foundation for the art of ministering to them both, but as he was pioneering a knowledge of political anatomy he would, like a medical student, practise upon a 'Political Animal', in this case Ireland (Petty 1691: Preface).

A proximate inspiration for physiological analogies was William Harvey's breakthrough studies on the circulation of blood. Harvey claimed to have identified the 'continuous and uninterrupted movement of blood from the heart through the arteries to the body as a whole, and likewise back from that body as a whole' (Harvey 1963 [1636]: 115). The imagery offered many options, and so an author could describe the way money circulated the state's trade and as acted as lubricating fat in the same breath; Mildmay, for example, moved freely between the beneficial circulation of money and its ability to overburden the stomach like too much food (Mildmay 1765, 115). Hobbes, who studied anatomy with Petty and was friends with Harvey (Aubrey 1975: 159), developed one of the richest analogies. He combined the images of blood and food, describing money as a 'Concoction' of commodities that allowed them to be 'reserved for Nourishment in time to come', and therefore like blood: 'naturall Bloud is in like manner made of the fruits of the Earth; and circulating, nourisheth by the way, every Member of the Body of Man'. Crucial for state strength was the ability of gold and silver to 'make Common-wealths move, and stretch out their armes, when need is, into forraign Countries; and supply . . . whole Armies with Provision'. The public treasurers were the heart of the body, who received taxes and reissued them through public spending (Hobbes 1991 [1651]: 174–5). The complex process of circulation was also susceptible to various maladies, such as obstructions and congealments (ibid.: 229).

The point to take from the physiological analogy is that trade was not imagined as something that happened in a space outside or alongside the state, like the economy is thought of today, but was rather the very matter of the state. Hobbes's *Leviathan* was a treatise on the nature of political obligation, and it clearly belongs to a genre different to counsel on trade but, as we saw in our discussion of genres of counsel, the common denominator was the position of the state as the object these genres apprehended. Corruptions of trade could be presented accordingly as corruptions of the body politic, and here we can note four recurring anxieties expressed in relation to circulation.

One was that the circulating matter itself was corrupted. Davenant bemoaned the effect of clipping on the national coin. Clipping involved trimming small pieces off coins that could then be melted down into bullion and sold. The practice caused a distinction to be made between heavy and light money, thereby undermining the role of coin as an efficient medium of exchange. Starting from the claim that 'Trade and Money are like Blood and Serum, which tho Different Juices, yet runn through the veines mingled together', Davenant could then describe the corruption of the coin as 'a dangerous Ulcer in the Body Politick', which required 'mending the whole Mass of Blood which is corrupted' (Davenant 1942 [1695]: 8).

The second anxiety commonly expressed in relation to circulation was that some of the circulating material might fail to circulate, giving rise to Hobbes's agues and pleurisie, or, if water was the favoured metaphor instead of blood, causing stagnant pools. Locke described stagnancy as an inevitable fact of the circulation of money, 'some of it will unavoidably be dreined into standing pools' (hoarding, for example), and this represented a straightforward diminution of trade because of the role of money in 'driving the several Wheels of Trade' (Locke 1991: Vol. I: 233). This conceptual framework undergirded many of the proposals for a national bank, including William Paterson's, who enjoys fame as the founder of the Bank of England. Paterson argued that one way a bank could 'facilitate the circulation of Money' was by minimizing its accumulation into stagnant pools, including those inside the Bank. The Bank would 'circulate their Fundation of *Twelve hundred Thousand Pounds*, without having more than *Two* or *Three Hundred Thousand Pounds* lying dead at one time', helpfully lowering the rate of interest in the process (Paterson 1694: 13–15).

The third and most significant concern that arose in relation to circulation was that some of the circulating material might perish or be consumed in the course of its travels between the different parts of the territory or political body. This line of thinking provided one of the strongest arguments for privileging the flow of bullion into the territory as an objective for governmental action. We have already seen how writers such as Hume claimed that bullion was valuable to the public in times of national danger because it made it possible to hire mercenaries and supply armies. The more powerful argument for bullion was that given its non-perishable character it permanently augmented a state's circulation by driving the wheels of trade, to use Locke's phrase. We can therefore note here, as others have already (Foucault 2002: 192–3; Tribe 1978: 88), that the so-called confusion between money and wealth that was supposedly typical of this literature is an effect of reading these texts through an alien conceptual grid. In Hobbes's imagery, bullion is the blood of the state that *spreads* nourishment to its different parts, but the actual nourishment comes from commodities; there was no confusion.

It was with these arguments that John Pollexfen took aim at the East India Company in his *England and East-India Inconsistent in their Manufactures*. Pollexfen claimed that no trade that saw perishables exchanged for perishables was harmful to the state, because both products would ultimately cease to circulate. By contrast, in trades where bullion was exchanged for perishables, the public saw the loss of 'what is durable, and most useful, for what cannot long do us any Service'. The relevant maxim for government was therefore that 'no Trade ought to be incouraged that is carried on by the Exportation of our Bullion'. Pollexfen immediately nominated some telling exceptions to this rule, for example: goods could be purchased with bullion when they were necessary for defence, or when there was an 'undoubted indisputable assurance' that the goods purchased would be exchanged for an even greater quantity of bullion (Pollexfen 1697: 49, 52).

With this last caveat Pollexfen opened the door to a persistent uncertainty in the analysis of circulation. This uncertainty stemmed from asking a specific question of a process that was represented as complex and continuous: 'does this particular trade increase the quantity of bullion?' Such uncertainty was hard to banish because it could always be claimed that the process of circulation had not been traced far enough (through enough veins and arteries), or for long enough (through a sufficient number of cycles). Pollexfen acknowledged this uncertainty when he likened the difficulty of giving a true account of 'the Turnings, Windings, Circulations, Steps, Degrees and Progress of Trade' in the political body to tracing the circulation of blood in the natural body. He then set this challenge to the side by claiming that there were 'some plain Cases relating to both', of which the East India trade was one (ibid.: 56).

Formulations of the balance of trade doctrine, such as we saw Thomas Mun provide in Chapter 2, can be construed as ending the uncertainty around the circulation of wealth by setting out a rule – the balance of trade – that could guide statesmen more simply than complicated representations of the process of circulation.[4] But such rules were challenged by assertions of the problem of perishability in circulation, such that not all traded goods were equal, as the balance of trade suggested. More plainly, a hierarchy could be established even among perishable goods, and this is the context in which debates over luxury and trade should be seen, for luxury goods were usually considered to occupy the lowest rung on the hierarchy of perishables.

Luxury goods were straightforwardly dangerous to the state because they did not add to its military might and they perished in consumption. The favourite targets were food and clothes, as evidenced by Samuel Fortrey's three-page list of luxuries organized under 16 different heads, four of which related to food and drink and six to clothing. Fortrey's solution was for his Majesty to commend local goods over imported fashions by his own example (Fortrey 1713: 17–20). Mun also focused on 'diet and rayment', but recommended the more common expedient of enforcing 'good laws as are strictly practised in other Countries' (Mun 1928 [1664]: 7), similar to John Law's argument that consumption was not the fault of merchants who imported luxury items but 'the Fault of the Government, who ought to hinder the too great Consumption of Foreign Goods ... by making the Vent less profitable at Home than Abroad' (Law 1720: 15–16).

Regulating luxury in this manner was challenged on two fronts. One related to the projection of the English as a people 'accustom'd to Mild Laws, and a loose Administration', who could 'never indure that Severity' that sumptuary laws imposed on everyday life (Davenant 1696: 48–9).[5] The second type of challenge related to the dangers involved in attempting to regulate a process as complex as circulation, which was a 'matter of great delicacy, and requires a nice judgement', because laws could be 'productive of effects, contrary to their intention'. Identifying this regulatory difficulty went hand in hand with the claim that luxury was not necessarily as great an evil as some authors were given to suggest. After all, luxury 'encourages the arts, whets the inventions of men, and finds employments for more of our own people'. Thus, so long as luxury only fed the vanity of a few, 'the ways of indulging it, should not be too much straightened' (Harris 1757: 29–30).[6]

Our next step is to consider how circulation was used to identify valuable sectors of the territory's trade. We saw earlier how Graunt claimed that knowledge of the lands and hands of a territory was essential to its government. A good example of this premise in action was Mun's identification of the two sources of wealth, natural (from the land and sea) and artificial (from manufacturing and trading), with the second source clearly presented as more important than the first. This was one of the essential moves of counsel on trade: to identify the sources of wealth and then discriminate between them, thus grounding programmes of action for the statesman in a knowledge of the workings of trade.

Jacob Vanderlint's (1734) *Money Answers All Things* was a striking example of this mode of argument because the land was privileged as the source of all wealth.[7] He made his essential claim in stark terms, 'All Things, that are in the World, are the Produce of the Ground originally; and thence must all Things be raised.' His policy recommendation proceeded directly from this insight: the 'more Land therefore shall be improv'd and cultivated, &c. the greater will the Plenty of all Things be, and the more People will it also imploy'. Vanderlint acknowledged the importance of circulating bullion but enlisted this objective as an argument in support of improving the land. A more extensive agriculture would make 'the Necessaries of Life cheaper', and this would reduce the cost of labour and hence other prices too. The result was that 'the Money, now circulating amongst the People, may extend a vast deal further than it now will do (Vanderlint 1734: 6–7). Vanderlint's counsel focused accordingly on the need to cultivate 'proportionably more Land', a task that was lent urgency by the pressing demands created by population growth (ibid.: 27). In fact, population growth provided a natural check against the over-cultivation of new land by regulating profits, the same mechanism that led people to be redistributed into non-agricultural occupations in 'that

Proportion . . . that the Nature of Things themselves would plainly and sufficiently point out!' (ibid.: 48). Here was an image of natural order built around the role of agriculture as the source of circulation, and it demonstrated how circulation was used to portray activities such as trade and labour as part of a self-regulating system. This is a point to which we will return.

We must emphasize first, however, that it was perfectly common for arguments to be constructed without using the concept of circulation. Most commonly, a particular trade would be identified as making an especially significant contribution to the state, a significance that derived from the intensity of the returns from this trade. Fishing was most often given this special status, as we have already seen in the discussions of the successes of Dutch policy. James Macburney likewise claimed that by mastering the fishing trade, the Dutch had gained in shipping, mariners, trade and fortifications, power, public revenue, private wealth, and their stock of provisions. Clearly, he argued, it behoved England to turn its attention to fishing in a similar manner (Macburney 1701: 3–7).

This mode of assessment could also be employed negatively, to argue that a specific trade had exceptionally negative effects: 'that a trade may be beneficial to the merchant, and yet injurious to the nation, is one of those maxims to which every body assents (Anonymous 1759: 224). Daniel Defoe lambasted the trade with Norway in this vein, in his *Review*. This was a trade 'driven with the most Disadvantage to us', for the Norwegians 'neither take our Manufactures, nor Employ our Seamen, or Ships', and these foreigners only rendered services that England could perform itself (Defoe 1965 [1705]: Vol. I, Bk III, No. 96: 397–8). Alternatively, a trade could be valued for the size of its contribution to a state's wealth. In this vein, one author argued that 'the Wealth of a Nation can have no other Original than the Product and Manufacture of the Country'. It was therefore clear that in the dispute between woollen manufacturers and calico printers – rival goods among 'the vulgar Taste' – the relevant question was 'Which of the Competitors are certain to employ the greatest Numbers most usefully?' The question was easily answered in favour of the woollen trade, which employed 300,000 workers in London and Norwich alone, as against the 800 calico printers employed in all of England. It followed that a 'total Prohibition of printed and stained Callicoes would procure new Employment for more than a hundred thousand People' (Anonymous 1720: 6–8, 12).

The limitation inherent in trade-specific arguments was that the trade of the nation could not be projected as a whole, but this shortcoming was avoided by combining trade-specific argumentation with circulation. Barbon, for example, made labour, or 'Industry in the Poor', the source of circulation, and so he evaluated different trades in terms of how many 'Hands' each employed. He was thus concerned with perishability in exactly the opposite manner that Pollexfen was in his attack on the East India Company. Clothing, for example, was exalted by Barbon because it perished so quickly through the vagaries of fashion, thus requiring constant production: 'Fashion or the alteration of Dress, is a great Promoter of *Trade*, because it occasions the Expence of Cloaths, before the Old ones are worn out' and this 'makes a Circulation' that 'keeps the great Body of *Trade* in Motion'

(Barbon 1690: 65). The usual treatment of perishability was therefore inverted, and this resulted in a demotion of bullion in the usual hierarchy of circulating materials due to the small number of workers it employed. In Barbon's words, 'Silver and Gold, are Foreign Commodities; Pay but little Freight, and Imploy but few Hands in the Working' (ibid.: 77).

The obverse move was also made, as circulation could be used to identify the constitutive groups of a population. In Philip Cantillon's (1759) *The Analysis of Trade*, in which he liberally borrowed from Richard Cantillon's *Essai* (see Groenewegen 2002: 188),[8] the circulation of money was described as payments between groups, such as tenant farmers and landlords, farmers and labourers, and merchants and manufacturers. The more frequently these payments were made, 'the quicker Money shifts Hands, and goes round', and Cantillon calculated that, at the current speed, only one-ninth of the value of the land and labour was needed in coin for its circulation (Cantillon 1759: 43). The ultimate source of all these payments, however, was the produce of the land, which was divided between the landlord, who received one-third as rent for the liberty of cultivating his estate, and the farmer, who took one-third for the subsistence of himself and his labourers, and kept the remaining third as his profit. Rent and profits were then circulated by landlords and farmers to merchants and tradesmen in the towns by purchasing services, equipment, and so on (ibid.: 114–16).

Having set out the source and path of circulation in this manner, Cantillon could then make the provocative claim that while merchants may appear to live by the proceeds of foreign commerce, they actually lived 'at the Expence of the Proprietors of Land, who live in foreign Countries' (ibid.: 117). And on this basis he could make two further powerful points. The first was that lawmakers should ensure that farmers and labourers enjoyed an easy tax regime to guarantee that the land was cultivated to the maximum degree possible, because everybody's welfare depended on this sector. The second was that, given the reciprocal dependence of all sectors of the state's population on each other, the distinction often made between the monied interest and the landed interest was not only false but 'very hurtful to the Interest of the Community in general' (ibid.: 118). Cantillon could therefore advocate for the landed interest and then deny their existence as such, all on the basis of his understanding of circulation.

Another variation is found in Daniel Defoe's (1728a) *A Plan of the English Commerce*, where trade was imagined in terms of circles. Every man, we are told, '*moves in his own Circle*'. For the clothier it began with acquiring the materials and labour to work up his wool for sale in London; once he had sold the wool, he drew bills for his payment and thus '*his Circle meets*'. The merchant, however, '*moves in another Sphere*', which started with his commission to purchase goods, moved to shipping them overseas, and then finished when payment was received. The captains of ships occupy a different '*Orb*' again. All the '*Branches of Business*' could be described as self-contained circuits in this way, and the people in each were generally ignorant of one another. When Defoe came to project an image of these various circles viewed together, he put the circle imagery aside and spoke of the 'Plan of Commerce' indicated in the title of his work. In relation to the world's commerce, when seen as a whole, he described an unbounded '*Ocean of Business*' (Defoe 1728a: iii–vii). Defoe was therefore unusual in using the imagery of circulation to identify particular trades rather than trade as a whole, but the circulating elements – men, money, and goods – were the same.

To recapitulate the foregoing discussion of trades and sectors, we can say that multiple and diverging assessments of particular trades and policies were possible by combining the forms of argument available to counsellors on trade. Yet one could not write just anything; the forms of argument available determined the objects of thought. At the risk of simplification, counsel on trade strategized the strength-wealth relation using notions of specific trades or circulation. As we have seen, in practice there was also expansive elaboration and creative combination.

Counsel on trade was also characterized by a fundamental fault-line, and this was a straightforward effect of attempting to subject a complicated process – the circulation of wealth – to the needs of the fiscal-military state. In this regard, consider the state's perennial requirement for bullion to finance its wars, which informed innumerable programmes within counsel on trade. Counsellors on trade regularly presented this appetite for bullion as in need of being curtailed by the limits imposed by the nature of circulation. For Thomas Mun, this meant that the 'gain of their Forraign Trade must be the rule of laying up their treasure', because taking an excessive amount would lead to 'the ruin both of the publick and private wealth' (Mun 1928 [1664]: 68–9). Similarly, Simon Clement acknowledged that the trading nations had never been as strong as they currently were, for having never before had so much bullion they could never support such great armies and for so long. Hence, the relevant maxim became 'he that hath the longest Purse, will certainly have the longest Sword' (Clement 1695: 32). Wars, however, could cause a nation to export more bullion than it received and this, Clement warned, was equivalent to 'Convulsions in the body, the continuance whereof cannot but be Dangerous' (ibid.: 17–18). Likewise, even though Hume valued bullion as the master of mercenaries, he also insisted that it was 'impossible to heap up money, more than any fluid, beyond its proper level' (Hume 1985 [1777]: 312). These strictures were derived from the nature of circulation, and they existed alongside programmes for state strength, often in the same pamphlet or treatise.

With this fundamental point in mind we can offer the second part of our answer to how the needs of the fiscal-military state were connected with counsel on trade. The circulation of wealth was analysed as a complex process, and it was also analysed from the point of view of the state's need for exorbitant quantities of men, money, and military supplies. These diverging perspectives marked the genre with its defining torsion. On the one hand, counsellors were mindful that the process of circulation should be respected but, on the other hand, they recognized that the state would need to constantly intervene in this process in an instrumental fashion. This torsion was eased by the capacious and uneven character of the strength and wealth categories, which meant one could talk exclusively of state strength, or of the circulation of wealth, or combine the two concerns in the same piece of counsel without commenting on the difficulties involved. We are not, therefore, dealing with a contradiction, which the genre was bound to relieve itself of through evolution or transformation into political economy; a torsion is not as serious as a contradiction and can be borne indefinitely. Rather, the point is that the discursive tension between conceptions of circulation and state strength gave this species of knowledge its uniqueness, and this will provide us with a basis for distinguishing between counsel on trade and political economy in future chapters.

Conclusion

To bring this chapter to a close, we can compare this characterization of counsel on trade with Foucault's presentation of mercantilism, which was central to his theses about the emergence of the economy as a field of government and the concomitant rise of a liberal governmentality (Foucault 2007: 87–114). Foucault's historical material was organized by a schema that posited an emerging 'art of government' that superseded its competing rationalities, such as the art of personal power, which Machiavelli's critics found in his *Il Principe*. The art of government was distinguished by its tendency to treat the techniques and objects of government as varying with the domain in which government was exercised, and to which these objects and techniques were immanent. Machiavelli's cunning prince, by contrast, was only interested in maintaining his *stato*, his control of the principality, and this overriding concern determined his activity across multiple domains. The prince's reason was singular and so lacked the multiplicity that distinguished the art of government.

In the seventeenth century, the development of an art of government was hindered by two factors: first, by the military and political crises of the period,[9] and, second, by the prevalence of political thinking that presupposed either the model of sovereignty, such as Hobbes's account of the rights and duties of subjects, or the closely related model of the household, which we have already encountered in James Steuart's description of political œconomy. Foucault's concrete example of an art of government was mercantilism, which was said to represent an embryonic political economy that could not develop because of the second reason in particular: mercantilism was wedged between the model of sovereignty, which was too abstract, and the model of the patriarchal father's œconomy, which presupposed overly meticulous and detailed regulation. Mercantilism 'was blocked and halted precisely because it took the sovereign's might as its essential objective', and thus its instruments were 'laws, edicts, and regulations ... the traditional weapons of sovereignty' (ibid.: 102). Neither the object nor the techniques of mercantilism were specific to the economy, and so it did not qualify as an art of government.

Political economy did eventually emerge, and the vital event was the 'perception of the specific problems of the population' and 'the isolation of the level of reality that we call the economy' (ibid.: 104). That is, political economy was an art of government because its object (population) and its techniques (governing through natural bio-economic processes) were specific to the domain in which they operated (the economy). The discovery of the population as a theoretical object was crucial because this object was construed as a complex datum functionally determined by a series of variables. It followed that population 'cannot be transparent to the sovereign's action' and so 'the relation between the population and sovereign cannot simply be one of obedience' (ibid.: 71). Population, in other words, invalidated sovereignty as a model of government and thus required the development of a new rationality of government specific to the economy; Foucault presented political economy as this new rationality.

On the basis of the arguments presented in this chapter we can make two objections to Foucault's narrative. First, the clash that is central to Foucault's account, between the rigid, law-giving nature of sovereignty and the autonomous nature of the phenomena the sovereign would command, was already present in the literature he described as mercantilist, and which we are calling counsel on trade. This torsion emerged in the space between two contraposed imperatives. On the one hand, there was the desire to know what Pollexfen called the 'Turnings, Windings, Circulations, Steps, Degrees and Progress of Trade' in the political body, and the claims to have recognized the ordering force that Vanderlint described as 'the Nature of Things themselves'. On the other hand, there laid the need for the statesman to disregard these processes and instrumentally extract the elements of strength for the territory's defence.

Second, the torsion in counsel on trade was not of the type Foucault elaborated. Foucault projected a clash between divergent rationalities: sovereignty and political economy. In this clash, the economic subject refused its status as a juridical subject and instead asserted its economic identity to say no to the sovereign as lawgiver. This refusal was mirrored by population (the economic subject's equally recalcitrant companion), which confronted the sovereign with the technical limits of sovereign power.[10] Seductive as it is, this image of conflict presupposed a homogenous ideational space where diverse rationalities meet and do battle. The historical reality is rather that different rationalities are put to specific uses in restricted contexts. For example, it is true that Smith disputed trade legislation on the grounds that it corrupted a process best left alone (the allocation of capital), but this was an argument for the reform of trade legislation and not an account of the duties of subjects to sovereigns. Leviathan and the invisible hand were not obliged to meet, let alone duel to the death.

What this observation suggests is that, rather than being a mere stop-over between sovereignty and political economy, counsel on trade had its own specific mode of operation that is not reducible to either an expression of sovereignty or an anticipation of political economy. We can reverse our earlier claim and say that the counsellor on strength was also a counsellor on trade, because the elements of strength were imbricated in wealth. The statesman who would increase his state's strength was therefore obliged to manage the circulation that carried its intimate connections with wealth. If he could increase the territory's circulation, then its strength and wealth would likely have been increased too, but the relationship was not linear: it depended on which parts of the circulation were augmented and their effect on other parts. This was the challenging task for which counsel on trade sought to equip the statesman, and it did this by providing him with maxims, calculations, an understanding of sources of circulation, of beneficial and harmful trades, legislative programmes, inventories of trade, and utopian visions. None of these arguments, it bears emphasizing, were attempts to configure the relations between subject and sovereign. Instead, they were intended to aid the practical management of the state in one of its dimensions – its strength and wealth.

This is the perspective from which to view counsel on trade: as a species of counsel to government on how to manage the state in a threatening world of rival states. Towards the close of the seventeenth century, an approving pamphleteer noted that the king had asked for counsel from Parliament, his 'Great Council', which was entrusted by the people with their 'Power, Purses, and all other things wherein the Strength of the Nation consists . . . to direct the Money, Men, Arms, Shipping, and all other Advantages of the Nation, to the Defence, Safety and Preservation of the whole' (Anonymous 1697: 3). Here is a list of the elements of strength we have been considering. These were the elements that political arithmetic attempted to enumerate, which the analysis of interest sought to direct judiciously, and that counsel on trade intended to increase. These three genres were concerned with the state, not the economy.

This is the first and crucial step in our overall argument concerning how the national economy came to be separated from the state as an analytical object. We now know that in counsel on trade no such separation was made, or, that it was the strong and wealthy state that these writers described and for which they produced programmes. No concept of the national economy in our contemporary sense was produced. We also have a good sense of why this was the case: because the arguments that were used in counsel on trade were concerned with the state or the territory and its strength and wealth, and this was construed as a terrain for state administration. Certainly the fact of circulation complicated the statesman's task but, ultimately, circulation was a process that was understood to require the state to act upon itself and not on a distinct domain such as the economy. This understanding will allow us to perceive how Smith's arguments sat awkwardly in the architecture of counsel on trade, a theme developed in forthcoming chapters. First, however, we will look at the arguments that described the relations between states via the medium of foreign trade, with a view to determining if they should be regarded as primitive international economics.

4 Strength, wealth, and state rivalry

Our counsellors understood the political world in which the state existed as a threatening terrain of ambitious princes and confessional conflict that produced extended wars and uneasy truces. The balance of power concept made the security anxiety associated with this portrayal tractable to some degree, by positing a barometer of international politics that states needed to constantly monitor and respond to. The attempts of states to influence the balance of power in Europe raised the issue of the connections between strength and wealth because, as we have seen, these connections signalled that state power could not be managed in isolation from trade.

There were several forms of argument that discursively linked state action, trade, and external security. Some straightforwardly reproduced the moves used in relation to internal strength that we have just reviewed. In the international arena, however, counsel on trade was augmented by incorporating arguments from the analysis of interest, which posited the calculability of a state's behaviour through the study of its interests and situation. Other arguments disputed the statesman's capacity to manage trade in the direct fashion these analyses called for, in much the same way as the nature of circulation could be portrayed as disabling the statesman's action within the state.

In reviewing these arguments, we will studiously avoid characterizing this literature as mercantilist, and this will enable us to cast a cool eye on Smith's use of this characterization and its extended consequences up to the present. Our other and more significant task will be to recognize that these arguments did not provide a conceptual apparatus that delineated the international economy as a theoretical object, that is, as an object that was conceived of by counsellors on trade. This is the analogue to the claim made in Chapter 3 regarding the national economy; these twin assessments represent the first and negative phase of our history of the formation of the national and international economies in forms of argument.

Strength and wealth, trade and colonies

Writing in the first half of the eighteenth century, Daniel Defoe observed that the '*Trading Nations*' of the world had become 'infinitely superior in Wealth and Power' to the traditionally dominant '*Fighting Nations*', and that 'if any one Nation could govern Trade, that Nation would govern the World' (Defoe 1729: 3, 6). Trade was now essential to power, and William Wood could therefore claim that the '*Theory* of TRADE is a Princely Science'. A nation's chief wish ought to be a prince who 'may know the Grand Concern of TRADE', for its good regulation was the '*Key of Empire*' and the foundation of the people's 'Welfare and their Security' (Wood 1718: v–vi). Wood's comments invoked a rich set of issues that lay at the heart of the relationship between counsel on trade, the statesman's conduct, and international rivalry. We can begin our inquiry into this relationship by examining one of the most common forms of counsel proffered to the public power in this context, which was to act directly upon a trade that was thought to be particularly important for state security.

The wool trade was again a favourite candidate for special treatment, and William Webster presented its case forcefully in *The Consequences of Trade*. Webster's central claim was that Britain was in gravest danger of 'becoming a Province to *France*, unless we immediately take care to recover our *Woollen Trade*' (Webster 1740: 7). The trade's significance for the fate of the nation derived from, first, the connections between strength and wealth and, second, its special properties in relation to other trades.

Webster's arguments about strength and wealth were of the kind we reviewed in Chapter 3: trade maintained people, caused a '*Circulation* of Commerce', and drew bullion from other nations; men were needed to fill army ranks, sailors to serve the navy, and bullion was necessary to supply them both. Hence, it was clear how 'inseparable *Riches* and *Strength* are from one another' (ibid.: 8, 17). As for the wool trade's special properties, it possessed two. The first was the labour-intensive nature of its production, which set more hands to work than most other manufactured goods. (This emphasis on the quantity of labour employed is the same mode of evaluation that we saw Barbon use in Chapter 3.) The second key property was that wool was essential to the clothes worn by the common people throughout Europe, and the trade would therefore export large quantities. It followed that the effects of the wool trade were 'greatly more beneficial than any other' and, Webster added rather hopefully, if the wool trade were recovered, then 'all our People might be employ'd' and their wages 'paid by *Foreigners* in the Purchase of the Goods' (ibid.: 10–12).

Having established his case for the special significance of the wool trade, Webster proceeded to underline the folly involved in not only permitting the trade to be neglected, but in allowing it to fall largely into the hands of the French, thus augmenting their strength and power. The impending consequence of this situation – apparent to anyone 'who is capable of seeing at all' – was that if the trade were not recovered, Britain would 'become a Prey to that ambitious Nation' and its desire for universal monarchy (ibid.: 17). The necessary remedy was to prohibit the export of unprocessed English wool to foreigners, thus using England's control of the raw commodity to full advantage. For Webster, the possible objection that this step might have led to open hostilities with France was hardly persuasive. First, if this step were not taken, Britain would continue to enervate until it became impossible to stage an effective defence. Second, in the case of war,

Britain's neighbours ought to league against France to preserve the balance of power and protect their own interests (ibid.: 20, 27–8).

The feature of Webster's argument to notice is that recommendations regarding national security were built on arguments about the nature of a manufacturing trade. This was possible because the intermingling of strength and wealth was projected onto relations between states. In consequence, counsel on trade that was concerned with matters inside the state shared a number of argumentative regularities with counsel concerned with matters outside the state, such as the practice of isolating one trade as being particularly important. There are differences for us to notice, however, and they relate to the fact that the British state was composed of multiple kingdoms, colonial possessions, and trading outposts. This requires that we look past the comfortable familiarity of the idea of the state and register its historical variation, in this case, via the idea of a composite state, which signals that most early modern states were composed of multiple territories, not necessarily contiguous, and that relations between the parts were unequal.[1]

This idea complicates our exposition, partly because 'imperialism and composite monarchy made uncomfortable bedfellows' (Elliott 1992: 60), especially in the British case because, before the Union of 1707, English interests attempted to keep the spoils of empire away from Scotland. The other and more important complication is that the arguments we will examine about trade relations between the parts of the empire played a role in defining the British Empire; this is what economists call an endogeneity problem. David Armitage has provided an illuminating account of how these debates functioned in imaginings of empire (Armitage 2000, esp. Chapter 6), and so we can largely leave the constitutional issues to one side and focus on describing how the management of trade and security were interconnected.[2]

A good place to start is William Paterson's manifesto for a revived Darien venture, *A Proposal to Plant a Colony in Darien*. Before the Union of 1707, the Navigation Acts were used to favour English commerce by obstructing Scotland's access to lucrative colonial markets, and this led to the formation of the Company of Scotland and its failed attempt to settle a trading post at Darien, on the isthmus of Panama (see Armitage 1995). Abandoned by the Scots, Paterson proposed the colony again, this time to William III, and in his plan we can see how colonies featured as elements in trade-security strategies.

In his address to the king, Paterson described his proposal as an attempt to open a 'door of commerce', claiming that 'both worlds, the new as well as the old, do at this time implore your protection' (Paterson 1858 [1701]: Vol. I: 117). The security issue to which Paterson referred, and which his new trade would address, was the conjoining of the interests of Spain and France through the House of Bourbon, particularly in regard to Spain's colonies in the Indies. Paterson argued that if it was true that 'the fruits of those new discoveries of the Spaniards have, within the last two ages, made far greater alteration in Christendom than the sword', the impetus that the French would give to the cultivation of those fruits should be cause for alarm, because it would create the conditions for universal monarchy (ibid.: Vol. I: 119–20). Paterson suggested that England was to be thankful for the

Spanish approach to the Indies, which he derided as 'lazy, negligent, and unto-ward'. For if another nation had managed these colonies, one 'only as industrious as that of the English or Dutch', he estimated that the quantity of commodities produced from them would have been treble. Such a competent state would be in 'a condition not only to conquer, but even to buy what was valuable of the rest of Christendom' (ibid.: Vol. I: 127–8).

This was exactly where the danger of a Franco-Spanish union lay, for the 'people, arts, manufactures, and shipping of France' would see to the 'best and most advantageous means of employing and improving' the Indies (ibid.: Vol. I: 120). As a result, the union had given France and Spain the chance of 'gaining the ascendant in point of trade, manufactures, and navigation', making them capable 'of putting what terms they please on the rest of mankind' (ibid.: Vol. I: 135). Since the source of the threat was colonial trade, Paterson's proposed remedy was for a countervailing colonial trade. The specifics involved establish-ing two or three 'posts' at certain sites in Darien, each assessed in terms of various factors, such as access to seas, freshwater availability, and climate (ibid.: Vol. I: 139–45). These sites would be secured by a military and naval force, yet they were to permit a relatively free trade, be lightly taxed and open to all. This freedom would even be extended to the indigenous population, who would 'get an oppor-tunity and be induced to set up for themselves, and be for the future enabled to maintain the freedom of their governments and trade', but still 'under the glorious and easy protection of his Majesty' (ibid.: Vol. I: 148).

This two-tiered system of regulation was Paterson's central means for securing the Indies. On the one hand, the 'advantageous principles of a general naturalisa-tion, liberty of conscience, and a permission to trade' would attract the trade of the Indies, since it compared so well with the high level of restraints and prohibi-tions employed by the Spanish. This would be a large trade and, even when lightly taxed, it would furnish the monies necessary for a navy to protect it. On the other hand, the 'natives' would be enabled to 'break and shake off the unjust and tyran-nical yoke of the Spaniards' (ibid.: Vol. I: 151–4). In this way, the Spanish and French could be brought to a lasting peace because both powers would be denied the increase of strength needed to achieve universal monarchy, at the same time as Britain gained in strength. Britain would benefit not only from the augmentation of her revenues, people, and navy, but also from the allegiances it would garner from other European nations as they became dependent for access to the trade of the Indies. And this would be a strong allegiance, underwritten by 'having their ships, merchants, and other effects, as it were, in hostage' (ibid.: Vol. I: 155).

Paterson's trading post was thus ultimately a means for securing an imperial polity against its rivals, by managing its own trade and the trade of friends and enemies. The commercial, imperial, and strategic were inextricably intertwined in terms of both how world trade was read and how it was governed, and it formed a domain that required direct management.

Daniel Defoe's arguments in *A Plan of the English Commerce* also evidenced this managerial quality. The intention of his 'plan' was to secure England's trade, which had become '*the Envy of the World*', and to do this via '*new Nations,*

*who may be so planted, so improv'd, and the People so manag'd, as to create
a new Commerce*' (Defoe 1728a: ix). Defoe elaborated four specific 'Schemes of
Improvement in Commerce' for this end, and one was for England to transfer its
demand for naval stores and timber from Norway, Sweden, and the Baltic to its
American colonies. The chief obstacle to such a plan was that the colonies suffered
a price disadvantage because of the high freight costs occasioned by the distances
involved. This obstacle could be surmounted, Defoe suggested, by freeing colonial
exports of duties and, in time, prohibiting rival imports (ibid.: 349, 352). Making
the colonies the chief suppliers of naval stores in this way would offer a number of
advantages. First, Britain would no longer be obliged to pay Norway for her naval
stores with bullion because the colonies would accept manufactured goods as payment. Second, the trade would employ British shipping and become a nursery for
seamen. Third, the population of the colonies would increase, and in consequence
their capacity to absorb the British vent would rise too. Fourth, it would aid the
balance of trade between the colonies and England (ibid.: 357–60).

Defoe's improvement would also offer a number of longer-term strategic benefits. Britain's role as the market for the vent of the colonies would see them 'ty'd
down' to Britain forever by that 'indissoluble Bond of Trade, *their Interest*'. With
this point made, Defoe could then claim, optimistically in hindsight, that it was
mistaken to think the growth of the colonies would lead to 'Mischief' (ibid.: 361).
The other strategic consideration was that this trade would thrive beyond the reach
of Europe's attempted privations and prohibitions, like a 'Mill built by the Lord of
the Manor' that 'is kept going by his own Stream' (ibid.: 362). Defoe could then
set it out as a maxim that additional colonies for settlement would always represent
a gain for the nation's trade, and he did so by making full use of the substitutability
between strength and wealth that we have come to expect from counsel on trade:
'An Encrease of Colonies encreases People, People encrease the Consumption of
Manufactures, Manufactures Trade, Trade Navigation, Navigation Seamen, and
altogether encrease the Wealth, Strength, and Prosperity of *England*' (ibid.: 367).

Just like Paterson's scheme, Defoe's mobilized colonies as a means for managing geo-politics, including the politics between the colony and home nation. This
strategy was recommended to the statesman who needed to act on the complicated external terrain formed by trade, strength, and wealth. The interconnections
between these phenomena explain why the supply of goods necessary for security,
such as naval stores, was the desired object of programmes of Defoe's type, and
why the statesman's decisions regarding the government of trade were so complicated. This leads us to a vital strand of counsel on trade that provided the statesman
with reasoning apparatuses to aid him in governing the import and export of goods.

The management of trade

We saw in Chapter 2 that one of counsel on trade's closest neighbours was the
analysis of interest, and Defoe exploited the possibility for combining their forms
of argument when he alluded to 'tying down' the American colonial interest to
Britain through trade dependency. The two genres could also be combined in a
more thoroughgoing and explicit fashion to offer the statesman guidance when

weighing the balance of power issues raised by the strength-wealth nexus. We now review this hybrid genre of counsel to show how European power politics was rendered cognizable and manageable for the statesman.

One of the best examples of this hybrid was found in the anonymously authored *An Account of the Constitution and Present State of Great Britain*.[3] Britain's trade and security interests with respect to other nations were treated at length in its closing sections, and trade was considered first because, in view of the links between trade and strength, 'on that in a great measure depends our *security*' (Anonymous 1759: 223). Yet the principles of trade needed to be set out, we are told, because they were not well understood by the general population, especially the grounds on which to assess a trade's usefulness for the nation. The maxims we are given turn out to be of a typical kind, for example: a nation's strength consisted in the number of its inhabitants employed in manufacturing; the balance of trade between two states would be paid in bullion; manufacturing exports made solely of British materials were to be especially prized; the re-export and carrying trades were advantageous because they employed sailors and shipping; the importation of consumable luxuries using bullion was harmful (ibid.: 224–33).

These maxims provided the basis for assessing how Britain's trade interest was served by its commerce with the colonies and other nations. Trade with the American colonies, for example, was judged to be the most important because the colonies received British manufactures in exchange for raw produce that Britain both consumed and re-exported, and hence the colonies were 'a source of wealth and strength' for Britain. Colonies were not always beneficial in this way: for example, Spain's colonies were seen to have drained the population and left the land uncultivated. Closer to home, Ireland exported wool to France – allowing her to compete with England in that most important trade – and supplied victuals to French ships cheaper than to Britain's. In sum, it 'seems as if *Ireland* was held for the service of *France*'. The most harmful settlements, however, were those in East India, where few manufactured goods and large quantities of bullion were sent in exchange for luxuries. This negative assessment was compounded by the familiar observation that the East Indian trade was exclusive, so that the nation was burdened for the benefit of a few (ibid.: 233–7).

After making these assessments of the colonial trades, the author's attention turned to trade with other nations. It was acknowledged that the balance of the Baltic trade was against Britain, but this trade could still be justified because the goods received were principally naval stores and therefore essential to national security. This fact further required Britain to moderate the balance of power between Denmark, Sweden, and Russia, for if any of these nations were to become 'master of the *Baltic*', they would be in a position to damage Britain's naval power. This security risk provided a powerful argument for cultivating the naval stores trade with the colonies through their 'proper management', and then Britain would need not 'suffer herself to be dependent' (ibid.: 137). It should be clear that this proposal reproduced the logic of Defoe's argument for shifting the naval stores trade to the colonies, including the suggestion that fostering this trade with the colonies would ensure their continued loyalty to Britain.

The Dutch represented a more complicated case, not least because they pursued an 'imaginary interest' contrary to their own and Britain's, owing to corruption from French gold and the factious structure of their government. The author claimed that Britain perceived its interest on this question in an equally imperfect fashion due to the distorting effects of jealousy of trade. A second complexity was the failure of Britain's negotiators to achieve treaties that would prohibit the Dutch from carrying French manufactures during wartime. The combined influences of corrupt and false interests, and the failure to regulate Dutch neutrality, had led to a lamentable state of affairs where British and Dutch interests were misaligned during conflict, which in turn made it exceedingly difficult to humble France in wartime, even when her fleets were blockaded and her shipping destroyed. Looking past these obstacles to Britain's real interests, it was clear that the Dutch had to be maintained as a free state who would guard the balance of power from France's deadly ambitions, and since the balance of trade favoured Britain, this trade did not stand in need of urgent attention (ibid.: 247–51).

When the discussion shifted from the trade interest to Britain's security interest, France featured large once again: by aspiring to universal monarchy France obliged Britain to adopt a directly opposed interest. In fact, given the recent additions to France's commerce and dominions, it was necessary to take immediate action to preserve Europe's safety. Such action ultimately amounted to strengthening alliances with Protestant powers on the continent through subsidies and commerce. But two reserve strategies were also indicated. First, if the Dutch continued to be 'obstinate, inactive, and blind to their own interest' in regards to halting France, then it 'may be prudent in *Great Britain* to strengthen and create as it were other maritime powers', such as Denmark, Sweden, and Russia, who through commercial treaties and Britain's assistance could be made to 'cut a greater figure on the ocean'. The second strategy, which would be occasioned by the failure of the first, was to pursue an isolationist approach in which resources would not be expended on the continent but solely on securing Britain's naval power and trade (ibid.: 254, 261–7). In this example, the management of trade was connected to an expansive array of security calculations, strategies, and actions.

William Wood had earlier developed a similar analysis in his *A Survey of Trade*. The statesman's need for guidance was said to arise from the fact that, just as the 'Nature of *particular Trades* vary exceedingly', so too did their effects, and hence to judge a trade's good or ill effects on the nation it is 'necessary to give the MARKS of a *Beneficial* TRADE' (Wood 1718: 81). While these marks were various, they once again amounted to some standard claims that could have provided the inspiration for those maxims we have just encountered. For example, manufactured exports were beneficial, imports of foreign materials to be manufactured and exported were profitable, the balance of trade was paid in bullion, trades that reduced the subsistence of the people were hurtful to the nation (ibid.: 81–4). Some caveats and qualifications were then introduced into the analysis, including the need to consider that the export of bullion may be justified in certain situations, for example, when the goods purchased for bullion were re-exported in a sufficient quantity to replace or exceed the original outlay of bullion, or when the goods purchased were essential, such as naval stores from the Baltic (ibid.: 89–91).

When applied to Britain's trade with France, these maxims revealed that the French trade was exceedingly pernicious, for it carried out bullion in exchange for goods to be consumed, including wine, paper, and silk. Wood could then declare that this was a sufficient basis for the legislature to make 'a Judgment of *our Commerce*' with a view to 'discountenancing' those trades that were harmful (ibid.: 94–5). These arguments, however, did not warrant hasty action, as had often been counselled in relation to the Dutch. If, through fair competition, British manufactures could be carried to market more cheaply by another nation, then that was merely a sign of industriousness or good fortune, and neither justified calls for the rival's destruction. Besides, Wood avowed, it was the 'reciprocal Interest of *Great Britain* and *Holland*' to be united for both civil and religious reasons. Moreover, even if the Dutch were destroyed, their trade would not fall entirely to Britain but would be shared between several nations, including the French, their common enemy. It followed that animosity towards the Dutch represented a miscalculation of Britain's real interest, one born of prejudice and faction, and a failure to see that the 'World is large enough, to employ the Industry and Wealth of *Great Britain* and *Holland*' (ibid.: 107–13, 122–4).

In the two examples we have just considered, counsel on trade and the analysis of interest were deployed hand in hand, but it is important to note that counsel on trade was also imbued with geo-strategic concerns even when the analysis of interest played a minor part. As we have been arguing, geo-strategic concerns were built into the foundations of counsel on trade through the overlapping categories of strength and wealth, and this fact explained counsel such as Webster's in relation to the wool trade, which we reviewed earlier.

Such security concerns pervaded Thomas Mortimer's compendium for the statesman, *The Elements of Commerce, Politics and Finances*. Mortimer laid it down as a maxim that commerce was essential to security. A nation without commerce would be 'ever at the mercy of a powerful neighbour' because 'it is commerce which gives strength and security to a nation, furnishing it with a maritime power' by providing a 'nursery for seamen' and employing a vast number of ships. Commerce also underwrote the population's subsistence and a supply of bullion, all of which were needed to avert 'the designs of an ambitious neighbour' (Mortimer 1772: 108–9, 113–14).

If the power and prosperity of Great Britain were to be secured, then commerce needed to be carefully superintended, and this explained why the first 'great skill of a statesman' consisted in ensuring a stock of food and clothing for the population, and inhibiting the export of either before this was achieved (ibid.: 111–12). With this stipulation in place, Mortimer then turned to set out the 'mercantile maxims' that should guide the management of exports, and again these were of a familiar type: exports of manufactured goods were to be prized, those carried in English shipping were especially valuable, exports to distant locations were superior to exports to more proximate ports because the profits and number of seamen were greater, bounties could be used to encourage exports, the export of bullion was not a public nuisance because the balance of trade operated through goods and not gold and silver, plus paper money meant the circulation only needed an 'eight part' of the coin formerly required for its movement (ibid.: 114–18). A converse set of maxims to govern imports was then provided, and while they were more detailed and sophisticated than our previous examples, these maxims still set out common ideas. But the seventh maxim is worth noting: the importation of rival manufactured goods from countries that did not receive any exports was 'highly impolitic'; so much so, in fact, that the consumers of French lace should be considered 'petty traitors, and punished severely' because 'they enrich our natural rivals' (ibid.: 124). This was plainly an example of geo-strategic concerns inflecting the management of trade, yet Mortimer did not need to use the analysis of interest.

Mortimer did, however, couch his treatment of the colonial trade in the language of interest. We are told that Britain's naval and commercial superiority rested on its colonial possessions, and this pre-eminence would be endangered if the American colonies turned their labours from raw produce to manufactured goods, forsaking their 'true interest' in the process. Only 'folly' or 'blind prejudice and partiality' on the part of the statesman would allow such a situation to arise, since it would force Britain to acquire its raw materials and naval stores from other, non-dependent, sources. Mortimer described a 'glorious union of commercial interests' between the colonies and the mother country as clearly desirable, and noted that achieving it was well within the grasp of a 'dispassionate, able statesman' (ibid.: 148–9, 156–7). Looking past Mortimer's erroneous optimism, we can see that within the same treatise geo-strategic concerns were treated by incorporating the arguments of the analysis of interest, and by the unaugmented tropes of counsel on trade.

The obverse relationship between trade and security was also mobilized, that is, the security of a nation's trade could be presented as one of the primary rationales for preserving the balance of power. This was the essence of John Campbell's argument about the dangers that would attend a Bourbon prince acquiring the kingdoms of Naples and Sicily. He concluded that if Britain wanted to protect her trade in this region, then she needed to make war, halting the rise of the Bourbons to be 'absolute Masters of all the Commerce to *Italy*, the *Levant* and *Turkey*' (Campbell 1734: 31).

Viewing the arguments surveyed so far in this chapter, it is evident that the statesman was required to perform a range of actions to ensure the composite monarchy's strength, wealth, and security. These actions included identifying and nurturing particular trades, adjusting duties to discourage harmful imports, piercing received prejudice to discern the state's true interests, keeping colonial possessions in good order, and making war on threatening enemies. As we have been emphasizing, the statesman was taken to be acting on and in a rivalrous and threatening external terrain. We now need to consider a final strand of counsel on trade that had the effect of calling into question the statesman's capacity to act effectively in the face of the nature of trade connections between states.

The challenge to the statesman

Thomas Pownall, the former Governor of Massachusetts Bay, claimed in *The Administration of the Colonies* that colonial government could only be achieved successfully through an *'efficient administration'*. Regardless of whether such government was carried on by a Secretary of State or the Board of Trade, the key point was that the chosen office be 'sovereign and supreme' (Pownall 1765: 12–14). It was the practical limits to government of the colonies that Pownall was referring to in his comments.[4] We have already seen that in the domestic setting the complex nature of circulation threatened the statesman with a different type of impotence, and this challenge was repeated in relation to the external context. In *The Laws and Policy of England*, William Mildmay elaborated a series of maxims for managing foreign commerce, and he simultaneously cautioned that while such management might be essential to attaining 'riches, power, and security', it nevertheless required 'great caution and circumspection' due to the nature of trade, which 'changes and fluctuates with times and seasons'. Hence, the statesman must not only observe the 'first appearance of every branch' of trade but also penetrate its 'turns and circulations'. Mildmay did not disqualify the statesman's ability to act on trade in a detailed manner, but affirmed the difficulties involved, and hence the need for the statesman's 'methods and arts of guiding it' to be 'nice and various' (Mildmay 1765: 51).

A far more powerful challenge to the statesman's dominion along these same lines was presented some decades earlier, by Isaac Gervaise in his *The System or Theory of the Trade of the World*. Gervaise's *System* was sophisticated, and its explication needs to begin with setting out its four key premises: (1) gold and silver were each treated as a measure of value and means of exchange. All things useful or necessary had both a proper name and 'another name', the latter being their proportion to the quantity of gold and silver in the world, or price; (2) labour was the source of wealth; (3) states were 'but certain quantities of Men' and, as a result, states attracted money in accordance with the quantity of men they contained; and (4) a qualification: the labour or produce of a state was not solely determined by the quantity of men, but also by its 'Situation, and Disposition', which primarily referred to certain geographical characteristics (Gervaise 1720: 1–4, 24–7). Trade or commerce was thus properly seen as the exchange of the labour of one state for that of another, and the quantity of men fixed its size, which in turn determined the quantity of money. Or, more precisely, a state would possess the same *proportion* of the money of the world as its trade represented of the trade of the world (ibid.: 3).

This was the central proposition of Gervaise's *System*, and it was elaborated, with some variations along the way, in relation to credit, manufactures, raising and lowering the coin, and foreign debt. For example, if credit drove the money in a nation above its natural proportion, prices would rise, turning the balance of trade against it. The negative balance would cause money to be exported until the natural proportion (determined by the nation's quantity of men and situation) was once again achieved. One of the powerful effects of Gervaise's arguments was thus to transform the balance of trade from a goal of policy to a sign of the excess or deficiency of money, something that was functionally determined by an autonomous process that traversed the boundaries of states (ibid.: 10–11, 14).

It followed that the manifold programmes intended to achieve a positive balance of trade were not only misguided, but actively upset this process:

> if Trade was not curbed by Laws, or disturbed by those Accidents that happen in long Wars, &c. which break the natural Proportion, either of People, or of private Denominators [national currencies]; Time would bring all trading Nations of the World into that Equilibrium, which is proportioned, and belongs to the number of their Inhabitants.
>
> (ibid.: 19)

In fact, because 'Trade is never in a better condition, than when it's natural and free', any attempt to force it by law or taxes could have pernicious and unforeseeable consequences that arose from 'Countrecoups', or opposing forces. These countercoups to policy were always 'at least in full proportion to the intended Benefit', for 'Nature not yielding at once, sharpens those Countrecoups, and commonly causes a greater Evil, than the intended Benefit can ballance' (ibid.: 23). Thus, the second consequence of Gervaise's analysis was that the statesman seemingly had no capacity to manage trade successfully. There was even a sense in which trade, or 'nature', was to be left alone to manage the affairs of states. Given a certain population and particular characteristics, an unfettered trade process would correctly apportion the world's money while avoiding the dangers caused by unpredictable 'countrecoups'.

It should be clear that Gervaise's pamphlet was an unusual specimen of counsel on trade. The author acknowledged as much: '*this System will seem new, and contrary to the Notions hitherto generally received*'. The fact that he set out a system of natural principles capable of '*answering any Event in Trade*' (ibid.: iv), and in less than 40 pages, has aided his status as an anticipator of international equilibrium analysis.[5] While such interpretations are hasty, it is hard to know what status to give Gervaise because he produced no other writings. More important is the apparently absolute neglect of Gervaise in his own period, which could be plausibly explained by reference to 'material reasons', such as lack of patronage or the distracting effects of the South Sea Bubble (Hoppit 2006: 102). But we should not overlook a simpler explanation, namely, the pamphlet's jarring difference in the context of its genre, especially its effective disqualification of the statesman's ordering hand. As we shall see, not even the supposed iconoclasm of Smith went this far.

On the other hand, neither should we overstate Gervaise's uniqueness. His dangerous 'countrecoups' were similar to the contrary effects Harris warned of in relation to regulating luxury, and his recalcitrant 'nature' was close to Vanderlint's 'the nature of things'. More generally, this type of explanatory recourse to the natural world was not uncommon. Josiah Tucker, in his attack on the granting of charters and exclusions, conceded that a given trade may be 'overstocked with

Numbers', but held that the best cure was to allow the normal 'Rotation of human Affairs' to take its course, by which 'Dearness begets Cheapness, and Cheapness Dearness'. This, we are told, was the '*Course of Nature, and of Providence*', and attempts to intercede with it in order to remedy a temporary inconvenience would only produce more dangerous and enduring consequences. From here Tucker could make one of the polemical claims he was famous for: 'That an *Englishman*, notwithstanding his boasted Liberty, is, in regard to Commerce, still NOT FREE' (Tucker 1755: 87–8). In the context of Tucker's tract, however, we see that individual liberty still stood in need of direction from public reason as manifested in Christian policy and regulations of the type we are accustomed to seeing in counsel on trade, so that the '*Circulation* of *Commerce*' was driven both by a centrifugal force (self-love) and a centripetal one (government) (ibid.: 7–8). In other words, images of a naturally ordered world of Gervaise's type could be accommodated happily alongside calls for extensive state regulation.

The broader import of locating Gervaise in relation to his near contemporaries is to emphasize that appeals to the self-regulating powers of nature were not extraordinary. Neither did they amount to arguments for international trade to be left alone to regulate itself unfettered by the anxious policies of states (with Gervaise as the possible and inconsequential exception). Trade was simply too important to the state's security for this to emerge as a regular line of counsel. Under these historical circumstances, there was no great impetus for a conceptual apparatus that would separate security (strength) and trade (wealth), or allow a counsellor to discourse on trade without considering national security. Yet the statesman was presented with some limits and challenges that stemmed from the interconnections that were perceived to exist between trading states.

State connections

In this regard, David Hume is perhaps the best-known example. In his challenge to the balance of trade doctrine and his denunciation of jealousy of trade,[6] Hume claimed that 'states are in the same condition as individuals' because, just like individuals, they relied on the industry of their neighbours to make the exchange of goods possible. Britain therefore prospered by the trade of France, and this was underwritten by 'Nature', or 'the Author of the world', who distributed different climates, soils, and geniuses between neighbouring nations for just this purpose. As we have seen, Hume laid it down as a maxim that it was not in the power of states to amass money 'beyond its level, while it circulates' because of the effects of price competition between states, and this fact revealed that many of the extant laws were 'impolitic contrivances'. Not all of the statesman's usual measures were thus cast aside, however, for the industry at home and in the colonies still had to be encouraged by taxing rival imports (Hume 1985 [1777]: 324, 329). Here, then, we see the nature of international trade setting limits to the statesman's action, but such action was still central to how counsel on trade was imagined and practised.

The same conclusion was supported by Joseph Harris's *An Essay Upon Money and Coins*. It was by 'the great and almost inexplicable circuit and labyrinth of trade' that the peculiar products of different nations were communicated to the world and, as a result, 'the whole world becomes ... one community or great trading city' (Harris 1757: 22–3). Alongside this cosmopolitan image we need to place Harris's statist strictures, for example, that every nation 'should have a watchful eye over its foreign commerce' lest the public be impoverished, and that '[n]atural alliances, and natural rivalships, for such there are, and ever will be, betwixt particular nations, are also subjects of great moment to the statesman' (ibid.: 23–5).

The value of a state's coin was a topic that existed alongside and independently of the regulation of trade, and its discussion also allowed the constraints of international trade to be projected onto the statesman's administration. Barbon authored a pamphlet on this issue in response to Locke, and claimed that the value of the English coin needed to be raised. Barbon's conclusion was built on two key premises. The first was that the coin used in everyday trade had two values: one for its use as a medium of exchange that could be received at the mint; the other value derived from the metals which made up the coin, which could be used in plate, lace, gilding and so on. His second premise was that the value for non-monetary uses was constantly rising as a result of Europe's increasing wealth, which engendered an increasing want for gold and silver. When the value of money for its metal content exceeded its value as coin, then its function as a medium of exchange was compromised. It followed that '*States* have been forced from time to time to raise the Value of their *Coin*, to prevent it from being melted down' (Barbon 1696: 73). The nature of trade thus obliged the statesman to undertake this raising of the coin. Moreover, because the merchants of European states would monitor the returns they could receive for bullion in different countries, combined with the fact that there was constant commerce between them, there was 'an absolute necessity for the Princes and States of *Europe* to Raise the value of their Money much about the same time' (ibid.: 75). The necessity arose because, in the absence of such concerted action, the profiteering of merchants would cause convulsions in the currencies of Europe. Although Locke diverged from Barbon in his analysis of coin, he nevertheless expressed a similar sentiment when he wrote that

> it would have been better for Commerce in general, and more convenient for all their Subjects, if the Princes every where, or at least in this part of the World, would at first have agreed on the fineness of the Standard.
> (Locke 1991 [1696]: Vol. II: 413)

In the case of coin, the nature of trade between states recommended cooperation between European powers. The essential point to underline here, as in the previous examples, is that states were thought to be connected by trade, and these connections could inhibit the feasible actions available to statesmen seeking to manage trade for national advantage.

Conclusion

Counsel on trade directed sophisticated advice to the statesman regarding the management of trade in relation to the external world. Seen at large, this advice calculated the interconnections between strength and wealth in multiple settings: the acquisition and management of colonies and trading posts, trade with allied states, trade with enemy states, and particular trades. These calculations also interacted with additional dynamics, such as the balance of power and the analysis of interest, considered both at a point in time and through time, and the limits of the statesman's capacities to act on trade effectively. This is an impressive list of variables, and if we were to represent these calculations mathematically we would need a system of simultaneous equations. While such an exercise would be self-defeating in view of our concern to avoid translating these arguments into our own modes of argumentation, the prospect nevertheless points up the inadequacy of portraying this literature as based on an identification of wealth with bullion and core–periphery notions of growth. As we have seen, these notions were clearly present in counsel on trade, but they were woven into a web of advice for the statesman who must take heed of the dense connections between trade and security. In other words, only when viewed as proto-economics does counsel on trade appear to dabble erroneously in international trade theory.

For all these reasons, counsel on trade should not be construed as a primitive attempt to understand the international economy, and here we take our next step towards the broader argument being developed. It is perhaps worth remembering that we have refused the temptation to treat the international economy as a reality or referent in the world that economics can perceive more or less accurately. Instead, we are investigating the object that historical forms of argument made it possible for the counsellor to cognize within the context of offering programmatic advice to the statesman. From this point of view, we see that the counsellor was describing a world of rival states that were growing in strength and wealth and fashioning their power to cope with the current exigencies of European power politics.

If we take the international economy to refer to the production and distribution of the world's wealth, then early modern counsellors on trade tended not to think in such terms. Rather, they treated strength and wealth in tandem, with a view to their effect on security. In this context, there was no conceptual apparatus for projecting the process of wealth accumulation independently of the actions of states and statesmen, for the interconnections that trade was thought to engender between states possessed no ordering effects of this kind. In other words, the arguments of counsel on trade did not elaborate a process of international wealth accumulation that represented a third perspective from which the counsellor could judge the effects of state behaviour on that process. Instead, the interconnections between states were presented as restricting the scope of state action in some respects, but that is all. The closest our counsellors on trade came to the perspective of a world economy was in their warnings to statesmen about contradicting nature, such as Gervaise's *System*; or in their invocations of the hand of providence in distributing the fruits of the earth across its lands and thereby creating a natural basis for trade. Before the international economy there was rivalry, nature and theology, and it is therefore no surprise that free trade was not a programme that guided state behaviour.[7]

Part III

Political economy

5 Smith and the economy

In Chapters 3 and 4 we saw that counsel on trade was concerned with state strength and wealth, and that the intimate relationship between these two phenomena was placed at the centre of analytical attention. The counsellors who advised statesmen on these topics mobilized a limited set of arguments, and this set did not provide a conceptual basis for thinking of the economy as a domain separate from the state. Instead, activities such as trade and labour were construed in relation to state power via the connections between strength and wealth.

It was these connections that were broken by the forms of argument introduced by Adam Smith in his *An Inquiry into the Nature and Causes of the Wealth of Nations*. The effects of these new arguments were crucial for the future of counsel on trade, as we shall see, yet by themselves they did not make it possible to cognize the national economy. Smith's arguments described the accumulation of wealth within a polity consisting of moral agents, and they were intended to aid the statesman's administrative and legislative action in this domain. The portrait of Smith that we will develop in what follows is therefore of an idiosyncratic counsellor on trade.

Smith's new arguments

The best way to grasp the distinctiveness of Smith's arguments in the context of counsel on trade is to largely follow the steps of his narrative as it was developed in the first three Books of *Wealth of Nations*. The first aspect to note is the centrality of labour, which was signalled in the opening paragraph of the Introduction:

> the annual labour of every nation is the fund which originally supplies it with all the necessaries and conveniences of life which it annually consumes, and which consist always, either in the immediate produce of that labour, or in what is purchased with that produce from other nations.
>
> (Smith 1981 [1776]: Vol. I: 10)

In short, a nation's annual labour constituted its wealth, which consisted in necessaries and conveniences. Note the immediate difference from the treatment customary in counsel on trade: wealth was equated with a generalized conception of life's needs and wants, and no mention was made of bullion, ships, ammunitions or naval stores.

We are then told that the size of this general wealth was conditioned by two factors: first, by the 'skill, dexterity, and judgement' with which the labour of a nation was applied, and second, by the ratio between productive and unproductive labour (ibid.: Vol. I: 10). The first factor was examined in Book I, where we learn of the central role of the division of labour in the process of wealth accumulation.

The division of labour referred to the increasing sub-division of tasks in the production of a given good. This is the context in which we encounter the famous pin-maker who, if working alone, 'could scarce, perhaps, with his utmost industry, make one pin in a day'. When this task was divided into its individual operations (perhaps 18 in total),[1] each person, on a pro rata basis, could make thousands of pins in a working day (ibid.: Vol. I: 14–15). Smith explained these productive powers as deriving from three sources: one, the increased dexterity of a worker who had specialized; two, the saving of time normally lost from passing between different tasks; and three, the invention of 'machines which facilitate and abridge labour' (ibid.: Vol. I: 17–22).

Smith subsequently registered two limits to the division of labour. The first was the nature of agricultural labour, which offered limited scope for the division of labour relative to manufacturing. For example, many of the tasks in agriculture were seasonal and, consequently, 'it is impossible that one man should be constantly employed in any one of them'. This general impediment to specialization in agriculture largely explained why 'the improvement of the productive powers of labour in this art, does not always keep pace with their improvement in manufactures' (ibid.: Vol. I: 16). This in-principle demotion of agriculture *vis-à-vis* manufactures contrasted with the status it was ultimately given when Smith applied his analysis to Europe and America, to be considered shortly.

The second limit to the division of labour owed to its very origin: self-love led individuals to focus on the task they had the greatest talent for, and then trade any surplus with others who had also chosen to specialize. Yet 'it is the power of exchanging that gives occasion to the division of labour', and so it followed that the 'extent of this division must always be limited by the extent of that power . . . by the extent of the market' (ibid.: Vol. I: 31). The possibilities for exchange could be extended by accessing foreign markets, which then deepened the division of labour.

In Book II, Smith investigated the other great factor that conditioned the size of the annual labour or wealth of a nation: the ratio between productive and unproductive labour. Smith offered two definitions of productive labour, and this explains much of its vexed history among his commentators.[2] One definition was expressed in the language of capital and profit: productive labour replaced the capital that set it in motion plus a revenue to the owner of that capital, in the form of profit or rent. Unproductive labour, on the other hand, was supported from revenue and afforded no return. Smith formulated his other definition in a language unfamiliar to today's reader, distinguishing between labour that 'fixes and realizes itself' in a 'subject or vendible commodity', such as manufacturing labour, and labour that would 'perish' and not 'leave any trace', such as the labour of a servant (ibid.: Vol. I: 330–2). We will not enter into the debates over Smith's 'bourgeois thick-headedness' on this point (Marx 1951: 177), but instead observe some of the uses he made of this category.

The first thing that Smith did with the notion of unproductive labour was to point out that the 'sovereign ... with all the officers both of justice and war who serve under him, the whole army and navy, are unproductive labourers' (Smith 1981 [1776]: Vol. I: 330–1).[3] This was the mode of assessment that formed the basis of Smith's system and separated questions of wealth from questions of strength. Smith then used the notion of unproductive labour to describe the differences between rich and poor countries in terms of the ratio between revenue and capital. In poor nations the mass of the people were maintained out of the revenue of the rich members of the society, and this mired the nation in poverty because the process of accumulating productive labour was continually forestalled. In nations like England, however, the people were supported by capital in the form of wages, which rendered them industrious and thriving (ibid.: Vol. I: 333–5). Smith could then claim that the 'proportion between capital and revenue ... seems every where to regulate the proportion between industry and idleness' and, as a consequence, the quantity of capital generally determined the 'number of productive hands' (ibid.: Vol. I: 337).

We saw in Chapter 3 that Nicholas Barbon used the number of 'Hands in the Working' as an essential criterion for judging trades. The same benchmark was also used by the anonymous author who claimed that the contest between the woollen manufacturers and calico printers should be resolved in favour of wool, a trade that employed 300,000 workers in London and Norwich. We can notice a similarity with Smith's argument about the number of hands employed in relation to the quantity of capital. It is more important, however, to appreciate that Smith had raised the level of *abstraction* at which this mode of argument operated, via the notion of productive labour and its relationship with capital and revenue.[4] One of the consequences of raising the level of abstraction was that two forms of argument that were routinely coupled together – first, the number of hands, and, second, the process of circulation – were separated in *Wealth of Nations*.

To see this point more clearly, we can note that, after providing his account of the differences between rich and poor countries, Smith claimed that the 'sole use of money is to circulate consumable goods', and money would 'naturally increase as the value of the annual produce increases'. In Smith's hands, the nation's annual produce was wealth, and it was augmented by the man who defeated the 'passion for present enjoyment' through spending on expense, and instead acted on the innate human desire 'of bettering our condition', by saving his capital for a profitable purpose (ibid.: Vol. I: 339–43). Smith did not mobilize circulation to explain the process of wealth creation and hence its role in these passages was purely descriptive. This is how the allocation of capital by passionate and desiring subjects came to occupy centre stage.

The decisions of this moral subject were embedded in a typology of the uses of capital, and here we need to register two preliminary points.[5] The first was that a person could only sell their produce once it was made, which took time, so that in the first instance a 'stock' was needed to support the labourer for this duration (ibid.: Vol. I: 276). Capital, then, was seen as that portion of a person's stock that was not needed for immediate consumption, but could be used to set oneself or others to work. Further, capital could be 'circulating' or 'fixed' (ibid.: Vol. I: 279). Circulating capital changed hands or shape to yield a profit (such as a merchant's goods), whereas fixed capital did not (such as a farmer's improved land). Naturally, either type of capital was only employed when the expectation was for the sale of the work to replace the original capital plus a residual, or profit. The returns to either type of capital were of the same form: a flow of commodities, or the 'necessaries and conveniences of life' that comprised the annual labour of the nation. The second preliminary point was the role Smith gave to supervision. The ability to supervise the employment of one's capital was a significant factor in deciding where to employ it. This idea was mooted when Smith rejected the idea that the profits to stock could be thought of as 'the wages of a particular sort of labour, the labour of inspection and direction' (ibid.: Vol. I: 66). The role of supervision was made more explicit later, when the workings of this natural preference were discussed. For example, the man who employed his capital in land had his wealth under immediate view and command, while merchants could better know the people they trusted their fortunes to in domestic trade than overseas trade (ibid.: Vol. I: 377–8, 454).

With these two preliminary points in mind, understanding Chapter 5 of Book II, 'Of the Different Employments of Capital', becomes easier. Smith's basic claim was that not all capitals maintained the same quantity of productive labour, and neither did all identical quantities of labour make the same contribution to the annual produce. This typology provided Smith with a general framework for using productive labour as his standard for assessing different trades, one that had unprecedented effects in counsel on trade.

There were four general uses of capital: first, in procuring raw material for either use or consumption; second, in the manufacture of this raw material; third, in transporting the raw or manufactured material; and finally, in the retail trade (Smith 1981 [1776]: Vol. I: 360–2). Each of these uses was essential to the operation of the others, in the straightforward sense that they were practical steps in the production process. But these uses were also linked by each step replacing the capital of the previous one. Crucially, it was this second link that provided the basis for evaluating the contribution of a given quantity of capital to national wealth.

For example, the capital of the retailer

> replaces, together with its profits, that of the merchant of whom he purchases goods, and thereby enables him to continue his business. The retailer himself is the only productive labourer whom it immediately employs. In his profits, consists the *whole* value which its employment adds to the annual produce of the land and labour of the society.
>
> (ibid.; Vol. I: 362; emphasis added)

More precisely, the retail trade only employed one productive labourer – the retailer – and that retailer's profits represented the only value added to national wealth. Given this mode of evaluation, Smith was understandably almost as unenthusiastic about the contribution of capital employed in the next step, the wholesale trade. The manufacturer, by contrast, was praised for replacing the capitals of the farmers and miners who supplied raw materials. Most importantly, though, the manufacturer's capital set labourers to work, in addition to returning a profit on his outlays. Agriculture was then identified as the greatest contributor to national wealth, and this was because capital in agriculture conscripted nature to labour for free. In Smith's words, 'no equal capital puts into motion a greater quantity of productive labour than that of the farmer', because not only did the farmer's servants and cattle represent productive labour, but 'nature labours along with man' and 'her labour costs no expense' (ibid.: Vol. I: 363). Nature's fecundity was acknowledged and then reinterpreted through an anthropological conceit,[6] and agriculture was identified to the statesman as the most valuable trade because of the quantity of productive labour it supported. This assessment reversed Smith's earlier in-principle demotion of agriculture in favour of manufacturing on the grounds that agricultural production offered only a limited scope for the division of labour.[7]

Smith therefore claimed that, when the capital of any country must be rationed between uses, wealth advanced most rapidly when agriculture received the lion's share of a nation's capital. That is, from the national perspective there was an optimal and natural development path for nations to pursue, which would maximize their wealth and its growth through capital accumulation. This path was to first exhaust the opportunities for directing capital to agriculture, and only then move to manufacturing and other uses. For Smith, the justness of this schema was confirmed by 'the rapid progress of our American colonies towards wealth and greatness', for such progress was principally caused by the judicious circumstance where 'almost their whole capitals have hitherto been employed in agriculture' (ibid.: Vol. I: 366). Smith also noted approvingly that capitals originating in Great Britain supported the export trade of America, which allowed the colony to enjoy the practical benefits of the export trade without using its own capital to support it.

It is tempting to construe Smith's analysis as offering a straightforward policy dictum: favour agriculture. Such a reading would be hasty, however, because it fails to account for the fact that Smith developed his analysis of capital allocation in an historical and institutional manner. Smith's deeper analysis was premised on two points. The first, mentioned earlier, was that individuals were not only attracted by the rate of profits on stock, but also by the ability to supervise their investment. This was easiest in agriculture and largely impossible in overseas trade. The second point was that because subsistence was necessarily a higher need than convenience and luxury, the growth of towns was naturally limited by the growth of the country, or agriculture, since a town 'furnishes only the means of conveniency and luxury' (ibid.: Vol. I: 377). The natural way to opulence was therefore for the country/agriculture pair to lead and for the town/manufacturing couple to follow.

Once again, the American colonies were exemplary: capital favoured agriculture initially, which produced a surplus that succoured the modest development of the towns. Europe, however, had not followed this path. And so Book II finished by posing the puzzle of Europe's progress: given that agriculture was the naturally privileged investment, how could it be that in Europe the returns to capital in manufacturing and trade were greater than those to be had in agriculture, when so much land across the continent remained uncultivated? (Ibid.: Vol. I: 374–5.)

Book III offered an answer by way of an historical account of the formation of town and country in post-Roman Europe. Chapter 2, 'On the Discouragement of Agriculture in the antient State of Europe after the Fall of the Roman Empire', identified the engrossment of lands as the primary discouragement to agriculture. This concentration was maintained largely due to the law of primogeniture, which was used to 'support the pride of family distinctions', by enriching one child while beggaring the rest. The practice was a shackle on the accumulation of wealth because it created great proprietors, who were a class of people wholly unsuited to the work of improving the land. Improvement required 'an exact attention to small savings and small gains, of which a man born to a great fortune... is very seldom capable', not least because his situation and training had given him a 'turn of mind' that favoured elegance over profit (ibid.: Vol. I: 384–6). Thus, the country did not lead the way to European opulence.

Neither did the towns follow. Instead, they charted a path to prosperity beyond the subordinate role of supplying the needs of the country. The advantages to be had in the towns in terms of 'order and good government' were one source of this precocious growth. The towns coalesced around a shared tax liability, which lent them size and importance sufficient to protect them from the avarice of lords. As a result, those who could not protect themselves accumulated their industry and wealth in the towns, even when it had originated in the country (ibid.: Vol. I: 397–405). The other factor was the role of coastal towns in importing luxuries from abroad and exchanging them with the country for surplus produce. The country came to acquire a taste for foreign goods, which enabled their manufacture in the towns for local consumption and export. In sum, town and country aided each other's growth (ibid.: Vol. I: 405–10).

The commerce of the towns should therefore be seen as instrumental in the development of the country, and Smith noted three specific mechanisms. First, the towns provided a market for the produce of the country and, through them, access to overseas markets. Second, merchants who aspired to be country gentlemen would move to the country and improve the land with an appropriately commercial spirit. Third, commerce and manufactures supported order and good government in the country (ibid.: Vol. I: 410–12). This, then, was Europe's retrograde order; it was not an unsuccessful growth path, but it was still the case that it would have been avoided if 'human institutions had never thwarted those natural inclinations' that ordinarily fostered the wealth of nations (ibid.: Vol. I: 377).

We must therefore reject reading Smith's analysis of capital allocation as providing advice to the statesman of the type routinely supplied by counsel on trade. For, rather than maxims, the statesman was offered a subtle historical lesson in the unforseen effects of legislation and institutions in historical time, with no straightforward policy implications. This point leads us to examine Smith's novelty more closely.

Smith's break with counsel on trade

We can make an estimate of Smith's break from counsel on trade with reference to Hume's essay, 'Of Commerce'. Hume, like Smith, had until recently been fêted in the secondary literature for moving past the analytical errors of his predecessors, and ostensibly there were some pleasing parallels between their arguments – both charted the rise to opulence in relation to the roles of agriculture, manufacturing, and luxury. The key difference was that Hume's analysis remained tethered to the fiscal-military needs of the public power in a way that Smith's was not.

Hume noted the commonly held maxim that 'the public becomes powerful in proportion to the opulence and extensive commerce of private men' (Hume 1985 [1777]: 255). It followed that there was no conflict between the goals of state strength and public happiness. Hume set himself the task of scrutinizing this claim, and his central move was to divide the bulk of a state's population into two classes: husbandmen (farmers) and manufacturers. Opulence was then identified with the extent to which an agricultural surplus could support the manufacture of luxuries, something that was possible because '[t]ime and experience improve so much these arts [of agriculture], that the land may easily maintain a much greater number of men, than those who are immediately employed in its culture'. The other way to employ the non-agricultural segment of the population was to conscript them into the state's fighting forces: a 'state is never greater than when all its superfluous hands are employed in the service of the public' (ibid.: 256–7). These conflicting employments suggest that there was a clash between the goals of state strength and the citizens' wealth. Hume showed this conclusion to be false in view of two points. First, in the absence of manufactures there was no incentive to improve the arts of agriculture, because there would not have been commodities to trade the agricultural surplus with, and hence no stimulus for its production. Second, in such a dearth the army could not be maintained in good order, and so must 'either make sudden and violent conquests, or disband for want of subsistence' (ibid.: 261). Taking these two points together, the more appropriate perspective was to see manufactures as increasing the power of the state. For a state, manufacturing represented a store of labour that could be claimed without depriving the population of its subsistence. An opulent state would also possess an abundant stock of useful goods: a 'public granary of corn, a storehouse of cloth, a magazine of arms; all these must be allowed real riches and strength in any state'. The relevant metaphor was the camp: not a Spartan camp devoid of luxuries and tightly rationed, but one 'loaded with a superfluous retinue' so that 'the provisions flow in proportionably larger' as a result (ibid.: 262–3).

In Hume's essay, opulence and power were still in close communion, and the correlation between the needs of the fiscal-military state and counsel on trade was strong. From here we can make three points to show how Smith's forms of argument precluded this type of analysis. First, for Smith, wealth was a nation's annual labour: *all* its necessaries and conveniences and not just those that augmented the power of a state. By contrast, Hume emphasized the abundance of those goods that enabled a state to 'hold out' when at war – corn, cloth, arms, and so on, and the stock of labour that could be conscripted. Second, Smith made a decisive distinction between productive and unproductive labour. As we have seen, this distinction related to the accumulation of wealth, and admitted no direct entry point for issues of strength. In counsel on trade, by contrast, labour was valued as a generalized source of circulation, or as a store of fighting men. On the one hand, labour was important because it augmented the circulation that carried the intimate connections between strength and wealth; on the other hand, a store of fighting men had a straightforward relation to strength. Third, Smith's general conception of labour provided no basis for identifying 'privileged sectors' comparable to Hume's manufactures or Thomas Mun's sailors. Sailors encouraged trade, brought bullion into the nation, and could readily be added to the navy during wartime (Mun 1928 [1664]: 73). This style of reasoning was what prompted Petty to describe the seaman as 'three Husbandmen' (Petty 1690: 18). According to Smith's analysis of annual labour, however, sailors and manufacturers were just a species of labour connected with one employment of capital or another, which in turn sustained a greater or lesser quantity of productive labour.

Smith's arguments were not intended to identify significant trades to the statesman for legislative attention, and to this extent the presupposition of the ordering hand of the administrative state was rejected in *Wealth of Nations*. This discursive absence was symptomatic of the replacement of the statesman by the moral subject, who decided where to allocate capital on the basis of a complex decision-making process. Capital allocation required the prior act of overcoming the 'passion for present enjoyment' (that is, spending on expense), and harnessing instead the desire 'of bettering our condition' to save capital. From here the agent's ability to supervise their capital became an important factor in deciding how to employ it, and even then the perverting accoutrements of wealth could corrupt its judicious allocation, as in the case of great proprietors. This is the famed 'economic subject' as found in the first three Books of *Wealth of Nations*.

If we supplement our reading with *The Theory of Moral Sentiments*,[8] then we find that self-love was regulated by sympathy, which Smith formulated in terms of the impartial spectator. Smith claimed that a man may run as hard as he liked in the 'race for wealth, and honours, and preferments', but he was still obliged to conduct himself so that the impartial spectator affirmed the principles of his conduct, something that often required him to 'humble the arrogance of his self-love, and bring it down to something which other men can go along with' (Smith 1982 [1759]: 83).

Taking these points together, notice how self-love did not amount to a distinct form of economic agency; economic action was not a distinct form of action. Instead, self-love was a motivation embedded in a general account of the moral subject, one that was intended to hold for all parts of life, including those we would retrospectively nominate as economic. This is a point we will return to shortly, but for now we only need to observe that it was this moral subject that allocated capital and drove the process of wealth accumulation, and that Smith claimed this mechanism was generally superior to the ordering hand of the statesman traditionally invoked by counsel on trade.

Smith's preference for non-legislative mechanisms is well known, but what we need to underline are the effects of his new forms of argument on a genre that hitherto had been centrally concerned with the needs of the fiscal-military state. These effects could be observed when Smith came to discuss armies in Book V, in the context of the expenses of the state. A wealthy nation, we are told, 'is of all nations the most likely to be attacked', and so required some form of common defence. This defence could take two forms: a militia or a standing army. After reviewing some problems that had attended militias by noting the relationship between forms of defence and stages of civilization, and the nature of modern warfare, Smith concluded that it was 'only by means of a well-regulated standing army that a civilized country can be defended'.[9] He also maintained that in view of the nature of eighteenth-century warfare, a standing army engendered considerable costs, which gave 'an evident advantage to the nation which can best afford that expence' (Smith 1981 [1776]: Vol. II: 698, 706, 708).

This discussion differed from the usual treatment of state strength found in counsel on trade, where the nature of strength was identified in certain stocks and certain segments of the population, which then informed proposals for augmenting these stocks and segments. In this regard, consider the following passage:

> the riches, and so far as power depends upon riches, the power of every country, must always be in proportion to the value of its annual produce, the fund from which all taxes must ultimately be paid.
>
> (ibid.: Vol. I: 372)

Since strength was a function of tax, calculating how to maximize those diverse points at which strength and wealth overlapped was no longer essential to the analysis.

Smith did resuscitate the old style of analysis at several points. He conceded, for example, that if certain manufactures were necessary for the 'defence of the society', then it might not be 'prudent to depend upon our neighbours for the supply'. He then grudgingly admitted that this reasoning could be used to vindicate the bounties on exports of British sail cloth and gunpowder (ibid.: Vol. I: 522–3). This argument held a formal similarity with Defoe's plan for cultivating the naval stores trade with the American colonies, yet for Defoe generating recommendations of this type was not a qualification to the analysis but one of its key purposes. Smith's use of exceptions of this type will be examined at greater length in Chapter 6.

One of the key effects of Smith's arguments was to link strength to tax in this way, and in this respect state finances were a point of disconnection between *Wealth of Nations* and typical counsel on trade. Yet they were also one of the points of strongest continuity, for it was in relation to this topic that the statesman made his late appearance as an ordering force.[10] The statesman was most powerfully invoked in Smith's explicit definition of his genre – political œconomy 'considered as a branch of the science of a statesman or legislator' (ibid.: Vol. I: 428). Book V outlined the three duties of the sovereign under a system of liberty: to defend the society, to administer justice, and to provide certain desirable public institutions that would not be profitable for individuals to maintain. The institutions chiefly implied by this last duty were 'those for facilitating the commerce of the society, and those for promoting the instruction of the people' (ibid.: Vol. II: 723). In these passages we see advice being proffered to the statesman regarding the laws he must enact for the good government of the polity – the bread and butter of counsel on trade, the genre to which Smith made a distinctive contribution.

Conclusion

Having reviewed Smith's arguments about domestic trade, we are now in a position to relate them to our overarching argument about the emergence of the national economy as a sphere distinct from the state. The essential point to make in this context is the traditional role of the statesman in Smith's arguments. In *Wealth of Nations*, the figure of the statesman was partially eclipsed by the moral subject and its decisions regarding the allocation of capital. Along with the division of labour, these decisions drove the accumulation of wealth, which was conceived as productive labour. On this basis it is tempting to suggest that Smith separated economic activities from other types of activity, and this would support viewing Smith as an early economist. This temptation must be resisted, however, because the statesman's elision was only temporary; he was reinstated as the target of address regarding legislative acumen and as the organizing authority of the polity in which the moral subject operated. In other words, Smith's forms of argument were still recognizably those of a counsellor on trade. We can therefore construe the self-regulating properties that the sympathetic moral subject lent to the accumulation of wealth as a variation on the circulation theme in counsel on trade. While Smith's manner of presentation needs to be acknowledged as both distinctive and disruptive – replacing the identification of strategically significant trades with the actions of a self-directing subject – the defining contours of the genre were intact: Smith addressed the statesman regarding good laws for managing the state's trade.

This leads us to notice the other reason for locating Smith within a science of the state and not a science of the economy. Smith's subject was a moral subject, one who sympathized with the passions of other subjects, and not an economic subject as we currently understand the term. It is thus possible to set aside myriad readings of Smith of the type suggested by George Stigler's memorable description of *Wealth of Nations* as 'a stupendous palace erected upon the granite of self-interest' (Stigler 1971: 265); if Smith's book had a base, it was sympathy. Decisions that we are accustomed to viewing as economic decisions, such as directing capital, were portrayed by Smith as subject to multiple moral inclinations.[11] Others have pointed this out before, but less emphasized is the implication that in Smith there was no economic agency and hence no mechanism for delineating the economy as a distinctive zone of life: there was only moral behaviour. The ontological flattening that Gary Becker has pursued, by analyzing all behaviour using rational actor methods, has at least this much in common with Smith.[12] Where Smith did represent genuine novelty was in his separation of the analysis of strength and wealth.

This represented a profound alteration to the forms of argument routinely mobilized in counsel on trade, or, put differently, *Wealth of Nations* failed to provide advice to the statesman on one of the genre's constitutive concerns. This specialization/omission was continued by those nineteenth-century authors who adapted Smith's arguments for their own purposes.

6 Smith and the international economy

We now continue our examination of *Wealth of Nations* by turning to Book IV, where Smith applied the analysis of capital allocation to trade between nations. As we would expect, Smith's concern was still with how different uses of capital affected the nation's annual produce, but his account was coordinated with an attack on what he termed the 'mercantile system'. Smith redescribed much of the material we have been calling counsel on trade as mercantilist, and both his label and the caricature it conveyed have been enduring.

Our task in what follows is to come to terms with Smith's analysis of international trade and the occluding effects of his polemical construction, mercantilism. In sum, and following on from our account in Chapter 5, Smith transposed the arguments of counsel on trade into his own distinctive key. He consequently ignored the geo-political character of counsel on trade and instead construed its arguments as failing to correctly analyse the allocation of capital as set down in his system. Smith's account was polemically anachronistic, but it does point us towards his difference, namely, that he projected the accumulation of wealth onto trade between states without the military-mercantile strategizing found in previous authors. Smith's intervention had profound conceptual effects: his new arguments made it possible for the counsellor on trade to accede to the international economy as an object of thought, considered as the site of the accumulation of the world's wealth and as providing a basis from which to judge the actions of states. Thus, with Smith, we take an important step towards our goal of providing a critical history of the international economy.

The analysis of overseas trade

In Chapter 5, we saw that Smith's analysis of capital allocation had several distinctive features. The first and most important was the relatively high level of abstraction at which it operated, and this was an effect of the general character of his two categories productive and unproductive labour. A second point of difference from previous counsel on trade was the notion that the ability to supervise the employment of capital – straightforward in agriculture, difficult in overseas trade – was important when deciding on its allocation. When this fact was combined with Smith's claim that agriculture represented the most productive use of capital, a hierarchy of capital employments emerged in which overseas trade occupied a lowly place. It is Smith's treatment of this application of capital that now becomes the focus for our inquiry. We need to begin by returning to Book II and noting three details of his schema for assessing the allocation of capital.

The first of these details is the geographical component of Smith's analysis. It was not enough to ask after the quantity of productive labour that a given capital set to work because the location of that labour and capital was also of telling significance from the nation's perspective. For example, capital employed in the agriculture of a nation must necessarily reside in that nation; the capital employed in wholesale trade, by contrast, could 'wander about from place to place, according as it can either buy cheap or sell dear' (Smith 1981 [1776]: Vol. I: 364).

The second addition was to divide the third category of trade – the wholesale trade – into its three varieties. In the first, the home trade, the produce of one part of a nation was sold in another part. In the second, the foreign trade of consumption, foreign goods were purchased for home consumption. In the third variety, the carrying trade, one nation transported goods that were both produced and sold in foreign nations (ibid.: Vol. I: 368).

Viewing this typology in conjunction with the geographical concern reveals that the varieties of wholesale trade must be evaluated differently from one another. Consider an example of the home trade, in which goods from Edinburgh were sent to London and returned with English manufactures. In this case, the trade 'replaces, by every such operation, two British capitals' – one in London and one in Edinburgh. In Smith's example of the foreign trade of consumption, by contrast, a home manufacture was traded for a Portuguese product, so that only one of the capitals replaced was British. Finally, the carrying trade also replaced two capitals, but neither belonged to the home nation – as when an English merchant carried Portuguese goods to Holland. The only contribution this trade would have made to the annual produce was the merchant's profit (ibid.: Vol. I: 368–71).

The third and final complication was Smith's interest in the time needed for each capital to be replaced, which varied between different employments, such that speedy circulations of capital were to be privileged. In the home trade, for example, capital could be 'sent out and returned' as much as four times a year, while in the foreign trade of consumption it could take as much as three years. In this case, the same quantity of capital employed in the home trade would have made 'twelve operations' as against one by the foreign trade of consumption. In consequence, and remembering that the home trade always replaced two British capitals, Smith could claim that the home trade would 'give four and twenty times more encouragement and support to the industry of the country' (ibid.: Vol. I: 368–9).

Smith's analysis strikes the contemporary reader as bizarre,[1] but we must hold to our methodological principle of suspending the question of the truth value of different forms of argument and limit our inquiry to investigating their effects. The point to make is that Smith used this geographical-temporal analysis of capital allocation to erect a hierarchy between the three sub-divisions of the wholesale trade, just as he did between the general divisions of agriculture, manufacturing, wholesale, and retail trade. In this hierarchy, overseas trade (which comprised the foreign trade of consumption and the carrying trade) was identified as the least valuable variety of the least valuable employment of capital.

This was not to say that overseas trade was an evil. Quite the contrary: when the direction of capital to overseas trade was a natural outcome of the progress of opulence, its effects were 'not only advantageous, but necessary and unavoidable'. Overseas trade permitted a nation's surplus produce to be exchanged for foreign goods, and in this way the surplus could 'acquire a value' sufficient to support the expense of its production. In other words, when a nation's capital stock had grown beyond what was necessary to drive productive labour at home, it 'naturally disgorges itself into the carrying trade'. It followed that those statesmen who had supported the carrying trade through various legislative measures 'seem to have mistaken the effect and symptom for the cause' (ibid.: Vol. I: 372–3).

In these claims we have the substance of Smith's attack on the arguments typical of counsel on trade, which he labelled the 'mercantile system' in Book IV. The assault derived its power from Smith's new mode of evaluating trades based on the accumulation of productive labour. In other words, Smith's new analytical engine led the assault on mercantilism by providing a sophisticated framework for portraying trade as more or less important for wealth accumulation, and for evaluating policies as more or less harmful to that process. Smith also deployed several cunning rhetorical moves relating to the relationship between strength and wealth.

The most important of these moves aimed to neutralize a customary line of argument in counsel on trade – that overseas trade was of vital importance to the state because it acted as a nursery for seamen and increased shipping. Smith acknowledged the veracity of this claim in his discussion of the carrying trade, writing that Britain's 'defence and security' depended on 'sailors and shipping'. We are told, however, that the quantity of shipping a trade employed was determined by the bulk of the goods and the distance involved. This explained why, for example, the coal trade from Newcastle to London 'employs more shipping than all the carrying trade of England'. Legislation that diverted capital from this employment to the colonial carrying trade could therefore reduce overall shipping, an effect directly contrary to its intention (ibid.: Vol. I: 371).

Smith was offering a cautionary note regarding attempts to increase naval strength through wealth, namely, that they could be self-defeating. This caution was immediately followed by the rhetorical triumph that we discussed in Chapter 5, in which Smith reworked the relationship between strength and wealth: power is equated with riches, and hence 'the power of every country, must always be in proportion to the value of its annual produce'. This was so because the annual produce was 'the fund from which all taxes must ultimately be paid'. Strength was now tax, a mere function of wealth, and no longer a complex category of its own. Smith could then define the object of political œconomy as increasing the 'riches and power' of a country, because he had redefined power in relation to the tax base, and therefore as one of the objects of his study (ibid.: Vol. I: 372). To the extent that his arguments excluded the usual meaning and analysis of strength, his definition was rather disingenuous. Thus, the substance of Smith's assault on those arguments typically offered by counsellors on trade was already substantially completed by the close of Book II, where the foregoing arguments are found. Book IV was primarily a sustained rhetorical campaign in which mercantilism was construed as an erroneous system. This, ironically, was one of Smith's most lasting acts, and the topic to which we now turn.

Smith's mercantilism

Smith construed mercantilism as one of two systems of political œconomy; the other was the 'agricultural system', or physiocracy, to which he directed less attention because of its lack of influence and the relatively benign nature of its analytical errors. By contrast, mercantilism was built on two great errors.[2] The first was a mistaken association of money and wealth, which led exponents of this view to fixate on a favourable balance of trade as one of the surest paths to wealth. The second error was the idea that a large war chest was crucial for supporting armies overseas (Smith 1981 [1776]: Vol. I: 429–31). In practice, these two erroneous notions were translated into two types of restraints on imports and four types of encouragements to exports. The better part of Book IV was devoted to examining these practices, but considering just three will suffice for our purposes.

Smith first examined restraints on the importation of foreign goods that could be produced at home, in the form of either high duties or outright prohibitions. The effect of these restraints was to engross a larger share of the domestic market for the protected trade, which then employed 'a greater share of both the labour and stock of the society than would otherwise have gone to it'. Given Smith's mode of assessing capital allocation, this outcome was clearly undesirable because capital – and with it labour – had not been directed by a system of liberty. The more general implication was that the regulation of a nation's trade could not increase the total level beyond what the nation's capital could maintain. Regulation could only 'divert a part of it into a direction into which it might not otherwise have gone' (ibid.: Vol. I: 453).

It was therefore only 'folly and presumption' that allowed a statesman to think that he either needed to or could successfully direct the capital of individuals. The far more prudent approach for a nation was simply to mimic the master of a family, who did not 'make at home what it will cost him more to make than to buy' (ibid.: Vol. I: 456).[3] Translating this maxim into the international context meant that, if a foreign nation could sell a good more cheaply than the cost of producing it at home, then it should simply be bought using 'some part of the produce of our own industry, employed in a way in which we have some advantage' (ibid.: Vol. I: 457). These advantages that one nation had over another, whether natural or acquired through application and habit, should be allowed to direct international trade patterns. Wine could be made in Scotland, but only at 30 times the cost of French wine, which revealed the absurdity of the enterprise; the same absurdity extended to those cases where the cost difference was only a thirtieth. All legislation that overrode cost differences was mistaken (ibid.: Vol. I: 458).

There were four exceptions to this general principle, and they demonstrated the novelty of Smith's arguments. The first related to encouraging those domestic industries that were 'necessary for the defence of the country'. The Navigation Acts, which limited trading access to imperial commerce for non-British ships, were identified as a clear example of a necessary exception because the defence of Great Britain 'depends very much on its sailors and shipping' (ibid.: Vol. I: 463). The second exception to the principle of free trade permitted foreign goods to be taxed when the foreign country taxed the equivalent domestic good. The measure was intended to 'leave the competition between foreign and domestick industry, after the tax, as nearly as possible on the same footing as before it' (ibid.: Vol. I: 465).

Determining when the third and fourth exceptions applied was more complicated. One related to laying retaliatory restraints on the importation of a nation's goods when that selling nation had first taken similar actions. Such retaliation, however, must be aimed at achieving a mutual repeal of restraints, since the 'recovery of a great foreign market will generally more than compensate the transitory inconveniency of paying dearer during a short time'. This led œconomy into a murky business: such judgements did not belong to 'the science of a legislator, whose deliberations ought to be governed by general principles', but to the statesman who must make decisions in concrete situations, and often for reasons of expedience (ibid.: Vol. I: 468). The final exception related to the return to free trade from a situation of protection and, in particular, where domestic manufactures had grown to employ a significant number of people as a result of being sheltered from competition. Smith wrote that '[h]umanity may in this case require that the freedom of trade should be restored only by slow gradations' (ibid.: Vol. I: 469). And 'humanity' would stipulate that concern be shown for two groups: employees, who lost their means of subsistence, and manufacturers, who lost some of their fixed capital (ibid.: Vol. I: 469–72).

We will indicate the significance of these exceptions shortly, but to prepare the ground for that discussion we can note how Smith used exceptions to introduce national security into the analysis and considerations for humanity. In other words, security had become an exceptional issue, collocated discursively with humanity. To pursue the spatial metaphor, security was removed from the centre of the analysis of wealth and located alongside it as a separate topic. We are told that 'defence ... is of much more importance than opulence', and this remark indicated that the two concerns were distinctive (ibid.: Vol. I: 464–5).[4] Recall that Hume needed no such hierarchy because he collocated defence and opulence in the image of the luxurious camp that combined riches and strength.

The second mercantile practice that Smith set his sights on was restraining imports from certain nations because they were thought to win the balance of trade, which prejudiced Britain's accumulation of gold and silver. Unlike the practice of restraining imports to protect domestic industry, which grew out of the spirit of monopoly, a concern with the balance of trade reflected the influence of national animosity, especially towards France. This maxim was said to be mistaken even on the principles of the commercial system, because if cheapness were allowed to guide the choice of supplier, then the total import cost would be reduced, thereby improving the overall balance of trade. In addition, mercantilists seemed to ignore the potential for re-export, which could achieve a compensating influx of bullion, and the fact that it was exceedingly hard to determine the balance of trade accurately was also insufficiently recognized (ibid.: Vol. I: 473–9).

We should note the shallowness of Smith's portrayal of 'mercantile' arguments, which he presented as fixated on gold and silver instead of power management. This caricature was followed by Smith's more substantial attack on the balance of trade doctrine from the perspective of his own principles. His central point was that trade 'naturally and regularly carried on between any two places, is always advantageous, though not always equally so, to both' (ibid.: Vol. I: 489). In this context, advantageous referred to the contribution a trade made to the nation's annual produce. It followed that determining which nation benefitted most from the exchange required that the effects of the capital employed be examined in the way we are now familiar with. For example, if England traded East India goods for French wine, then a greater quantity of productive labour was maintained in France (in agriculture) than in England (in the carrying trade). On the basis of Smith's system, the fact that France derived a greater benefit from this trade was not an issue if England had come to direct capital to the carrying trade as a result of the natural progress of opulence.

This new logic threatened to dissolve the rivalry between France and England by transforming commerce from a source of discord into a 'bond of union and friendship'. As soon as Smith articulated this idea, however, he acknowledged that the wealth of a neighbour may enable it to 'maintain fleets and armies superior to our own', and hence it was only in peace that an unfettered trade with France could be celebrated. The irony was that, given the proximity of France and Britain, the time taken for the replacement of capital in overseas trade was greatly reduced, so that a trade with France would be at least 'three times more advantageous, than the boasted trade with our North American colonies'. Free trade was thus the 'real interest' of both nations, but it could not be achieved because 'being neighbours, they are necessarily enemies' (ibid.: Vol. I: 493–6).

Once again, Smith's comments on security were inserted awkwardly into the analysis, and we can note that the shallowness of his caricature of mercantilism masked the deficiency of his own arguments. More plainly, counsellors on trade routinely judged France to be Britain's enemy not because it was a neighbour, but on the basis of detailed and repeated assessments of the ambition of French rulers, the extent of its power, fear of popery, and frequent examples of French aggression. While Smith mobilized selected discursive tactics from the analysis of interest, such as identifying real interests and their occlusion by emotions and poor judgement, he nevertheless effectively erased the connections between the analysis of interest and counsel on trade. As a consequence, he was able to develop his analysis of wealth with unprecedented sophistication, but at the same time his ability to advise statesmen on geo-politics was impoverished.

Nevertheless, the effects of Smith's sophistication were far-reaching. Shorn of geopolitics, his analysis of wealth accumulation portrayed international trade in a new way: instead of the balance of trade, the new criterion for judging the decay or growth of a nation was the balance of produce and consumption. That is, when the annual produce was greater than the annual consumption, 'the society in this case lives within its revenue, and what is annually saved out of its revenue, is naturally added to its capital, and employed so as to increase still further the annual produce' (ibid.: Vol. I: 497). Unlike the balance of trade, which referred only to one nation, Smith's balance 'may take place in the whole globe of the earth, of which the wealth, population, and improvement may be either gradually increasing or gradually decaying' (ibid.: Vol. I: 497).

The accumulation of wealth was projected onto an international context that provided a hitherto unavailable basis for assessing trade practices – with regard for their effect on the *world's wealth*. Smith's arguments made it possible for the counsellor on trade to accede to this new theoretical object. We will return to this point shortly.

If we examine Smith's treatment of colonies, we find that they were primarily construed as places that advanced 'more rapidly to wealth and greatness than any other human society' (ibid.: Vol. II: 564). We already know why Smith would make this claim – colonies could follow the optimal development path by directing the bulk of their capital to agriculture, which made the greatest contribution to raising the annual produce. Furthermore, colonies benefited from modern techniques of cultivation, and could avoid institutional obstacles such as the concentration of land ownership and primogeniture, which hindered Europe's progress (ibid.: Vol. II: 564–5, 572). Smith's system also represented colonies as extensions of the market. Along with supplying goods that might not otherwise be available, colonies offered a 'more extensive market' for the surplus produce of the nations they traded with directly and indirectly (ibid.: Vol. II: 592). As discussed earlier, the extent of the market provided a limit to the division of labour, so that colonies could be thought of as instruments for pushing back a boundary to the accumulation of wealth.[5]

A second way in which colonies were portrayed was as targets of mercantile regulation, which had subjected their commerce to a slew of harmful practices, including granting exclusive trading rights to private companies, limiting the colonial trade to ports in the mother country only, and imposing restrictions on which nations could carry colonial produce (ibid.: Vol. II: 575–7). At the general level, the effect of these measures was to direct capital and labour by force instead of liberty, and Smith's analysis was predisposed to assess such a situation negatively. More specifically, when Great Britain established a monopoly on the trade of her colonies, this precipitated the withdrawal of foreign capital. British capital was consequently obliged to supply the entire trade. Smith claimed that this reallocation had occurred in part through the diversion of capital that was engaged in a British foreign trade of consumption with a neighbouring nation into a colonial carrying trade. In the terms of Smith's system, such a reallocation of capital was inferior for two reasons: because the increased carrying distance made returns less frequent, and because capital had moved down the hierarchy of capital employments (ibid.: Vol. II: 595–6, 600–1, 604).

There were, however, two additional disadvantages to the effects described above. First, the monopoly on colonial trade led Britain's capital away from many small channels and forced it into one large channel. This meant the body politic was like 'one of those unwholesome bodies in which some of the vital parts are overgrown', and therefore at risk, since the loss of this channel of circulation would occasion great disorder (ibid.: Vol. II: 604–5).[6] Here we can mark the purely descriptive role of the circulation metaphor, in contrast with its typical treatment in counsel on trade, where the process of circulation was an analytical device in its own right, equivalent to Smith's typology of capital employments. Second, the high rate of profits created by monopoly 'seems every where to destroy that parsimony which in other circumstances is natural to the character of the merchant', and this decadence could cause the capital and productive labour of a nation to dwindle away (ibid.: Vol. II: 612).

Despite these negative consequences that arose from Britain's mismanagement of its colonies, the net result (the benefits of the extension of the market minus the costs of the misdirection of capital) was a 'greatly advantageous' colonial trade. This, at least, was the case for Great Britain, but the outcome of this calculation would vary from nation to nation. For example, in Spain and Portugal a more rigorous – and therefore more harmful – system of trade regulation was coupled with the even more pernicious influence of an irregular system of justice. The combined effect saw the colony trade of both nations make small or negative contributions to the annual produce (ibid.: Vol. II: 609–10). In other words, there were degrees of colonial mismanagement, and Spain was once again exemplary for the wrong reasons.

All these considerations moved Smith to advocate that Britain relinquish control of the colonies. He acknowledged, however, that pride and the interests of the governing class made this impossible. In principle, Britain would benefit 'in war as well as in trade' by abandoning the colonial relation with its dependents, in the form of a natural military alliance arising out of 'filial respect', and the commercial advantages of free trade (ibid.: Vol. II: 616–17). As a more realistic proposal,[7] Smith advocated a union with the colonies, based in part on the idea that an 'assembly which deliberates and decides concerning the affairs of every part of the empire, in order to be properly informed, ought certainly to have representatives from every part of it' (ibid.: Vol. II: 624). In addition to this argument for the need for local knowledge, Smith spelled out the drastic fiscal implications of American growth: colonial contributions to the Empire's taxes might, in 'little more than a century', surpass Britain's. In this case, 'the seat of the Empire would then naturally remove itself' to America (ibid.: Vol. II: 625–6).

What we can see in these comments is the overriding extent to which Smith coded the external world in terms of wealth, rather than power. Indeed, Smith suggested that the discovery of America and of a passage to the East Indies via the Cape of Good Hope constituted 'the two greatest and most important events recorded in the history of mankind'. While he conceded that the full consequences of these discoveries were unknown, it was nonetheless clear that they had enabled distant nations to 'relieve one another's wants, to increase one another's enjoyments, and to encourage one another's industry', and were therefore likely to be beneficial (ibid.: Vol. II: 626). Against these commercial benefits, Smith placed the enormous injustices suffered by indigenous populations. More hopefully, the communication of knowledge and various arts – a normal consequence of commerce – might ultimately establish an equality of military force between the new world and the old. An equality of this kind 'can alone overawe the injustice of independent nations into some sort of respect for the rights of one another' (ibid.: Vol. II: 626–7). It would seem, then, that the rise of trade entailed an international destiny of opulent, powerful, and therefore mutually regulating nations. This was Smith's ultimate and optimistic rendering of the world, and it was unlike the portrait of antagonism typically produced by counsel on trade. It is the nature and significance of this divergence that we now investigate.

Smith's break with counsel on trade

Our examination of Smith's break with counsel on trade can begin with his exceptions to a general free trade. Smith's support of the Navigation Acts in the name of national defence was, on the surface, a continuation of arguments familiar to counsel on trade. As Hont put it, Smith 'did not hesitate to endorse the political protection of trade if it genuinely served national security' (Hont 2005: 53). This is true, but the difference was that Smith's analysis must be *interrupted*, through the device of exceptions, to bring the question of national defence into view as occasion required. In typical counsel on trade, by contrast, questions of wealth were already questions of strength and defence because of the inter-intrusion of these categories. This discursive feature was not carried forward by Smith's alternative categories of productive and unproductive labour.

This discursive isolation of the analysis of wealth could also be seen in Smith's exception for taxing foreign goods. This device was permitted if it could help to achieve a situation of competitive equality. Taxes were typically recommended in counsel on trade to promote privileged trades – such as the wool trade, because it was thought to employ a great quantity of men – at the expense of a rival nation. In *Wealth of Nations*, by contrast, neutrality was the new yardstick, because it maximized the annual produce. From the perspective of counsel on trade, neutrality was an incredible ideal to recommend, since it was insensitive to balance of power calculations. In a similar vein, deciding when to apply the exception for counter-restraints was a task Smith allocated to the statesman, now that 'insidious and crafty animal' (Smith 1981 [1776]: Vol. I: 468), whose decisions in concrete situations would be remote from the general principles of political œconomy.

Counsel on trade was occupied by exactly the geo-political issues that were excised from *Wealth of Nations*. Counsellors made geo-politics tractable through a number of argumentative strategies, including borrowing forms of argument from the analysis of interest, which provided a framework for predicting the behaviour of foreign states in relation to objective interests. Such calculations were seen as central to the statesman's task of ensuring the security of the nation. In *Wealth of Nations* these concerns and the policies they entailed – such as the Navigation Acts – could be rationalized in an improvised manner, such as Smith's device of exceptions, but they fell outside the regular remit of the science of the legislator.

Thus, Smith's analysis had turned away from some of the counselling needs of the statesman, at least in relation to how those needs were normally construed in counsel on trade. This can perhaps best be seen in the final exception he registered, which was authorized by humanity. This exception would benefit branches of manufacturing that had enjoyed protection from competition, and should therefore only be exposed to free trade in stages to mitigate losses of capital and employment. By contrast, counsel on trade was centrally concerned with the continued protection of labour-intensive manufactures because the state held them to be valuable, either as a store of labour that could be easily conscripted, as in Hume and Young, or as a key source of circulation, as in Barbon and Webster. Smith's forms of argument were unable to apprehend the former rationale whereas the second was superseded as a means of conceiving the movement and accumulation of wealth. When we view Smith's elision of the conscription–wealth question in favour of the humanity–wealth question in the context of the ferocious interstate rivalry of the eighteenth century, his treatise starts to acquire a recognizable character, one that belongs to academic philosophy more than to the chambers of state counsel.

By divesting his analysis of geo-political issues in favour of isolating and deepening the analysis of wealth, Smith made it possible to assess trades as advantageous if they increased the annual produce. The key point was that, within Smith's framework, 'advantageous' only referred to the impact on wealth, whereas on the terms usually employed in counsel on trade, determining what was advantageous was a far more complicated process. In effect, answering this question required an examination of the nature of the active connections between strength and wealth, and whether another nation's gain was tolerable given the state of external rivalries. These questions, however, corresponded to a world beyond the state where the threats of universal monarchy and the miscalculations of statesmen loomed large. Smith's forms of argument, by contrast, configured an international order that was foremost a terrain of mutually advantageous exchange, and secondarily one that held the promise of an opulent future of wealthy and mutually regulating states.

On the few occasions when Smith engaged in geo-strategic analysis, it was not to advise the statesman in the same manner employed by previous counsellors on trade. Portugal was described as a 'very weak ally', cheaper to sacrifice than to defend, but this was in the context of his disparagement of the mistaken principles underlying the Methuen Treaty (Smith 1981 [1776]: Vol. II: 549). Similarly, the inspiration for the Navigation Acts was likely national animosity towards the Dutch, but through a happy coincidence this policy was exactly what 'deliberate wisdom' would have recommended – a 'diminution of the naval power of Holland, the only naval power which could endanger the security of England' (ibid.: Vol. I: 464). We can see that by studying state behaviour in terms of strategic needs and corrupting passions, Smith's assessment resembles the analysis of interest, but these arguments were set to work in *Wealth of Nations* for the purpose of historical reconstruction, rather than application in the present.

While the character of the international order that Smith described was relatively benign, it was still affected by various maladies. One was the self-interest of merchants. On the one hand, merchants would attempt to extract protective measures from their governments, which would distort the allocation of capital. On the other hand, the merchant's commercial spirit was itself vulnerable to corruption from great wealth and high rates of profit, which changed parsimony into decadence. Another malady was national animosity, such as existed between France and Great Britain, which also gave rise to destructive mercantile measures that shrank the potential for wealth accumulation. In short, the novel forms of argument that Smith introduced not only made it possible to cognize a new object – the international economy – but they also made it possible to pose a new set of governmental problems.

Perhaps the most important problem that Smith's arguments identified was the colony trade. As we described above, colonies were significant because they increased the extent of the market even for those nations that did not trade with them directly, and because their discovery promised to usher in a desirable *telos* for the world. Yet the colonies were a problem in their current form, primarily because they fostered the misallocation of capital in a way that not only retarded the growth of the world's annual produce but actually caused it to diminish. Since for political reasons the colonies could not be abandoned, Smith proposed a union as a compromise, which was not without its own difficulties. Colonies were an inherited problem, and one to which politics would block immediate remedies.

For a point of contrast, we can recall Paterson's proposal to establish a new colony in Panama, in large part as a means for managing a threat to the balance of power. Although Smith was hardly any better than Paterson in balking at colonization, in *Wealth of Nations* a colony was not understood in terms of geo-strategy but with reference to its rate of progress to opulence, which in turn required assessing the extent of its mismanagement and the infelicity of its property institutions.[8] This was a new typology of colonies, and a new grid for classifying European nations emerged in parallel: a European nation was described on the basis of whether its annual produce was increasing or decreasing, at what rate, how far its system of political œconomy derogated from a system of liberty, and certain institutional features, for example, how strictly the rule of law operated. Taken together, Smith's new categories had an administrative-scientific character in addition to their philosophical tones, which contrasted with the usual diplomatic-military focus of counsel on trade.[9]

Conclusion

We can now assess Smith's position in relation to earlier counsel concerning trade between nations. The target of his science was the statesman, who was given a raft of advice regarding legislative pitfalls and their negative effects on the accumulation of wealth. The strongest theme was that the statesman should adopt a system of liberty wherever possible. This advice was built on Smith's highly developed analysis of capital allocation between the different varieties of overseas trade. It was on the basis of this analysis that he effectively disassembled a whole machinery of tactics for managing trade in view of external rivalries. The new arguments focused on the employment of capital, and the ideal quantity of capital would be directed to overseas trade by the operation of self-love. In reality, of course, a mix of mercantile policies would artificially raise this level, since one aspect of the statesman's craft was recognizing when the benefits of reform did not justify a clash with the prejudices and interests of his subjects. At the same time, the statesman had to resist the temptation to think he could produce a superior allocation of capital to what the unfettered pursuit of profit would achieve. As for trade within the state, Smith is correctly recognized as a counsellor on trade offering guidance to the statesman, albeit with some distinctive characteristics.

Two of these distinguishing characteristics should be emphasized to convey the scale of the disruptions that issued from Smith's work into the forms of argument characteristic of counsel on trade. The first was his presentation of much of the counsel that preceded his work as the error-ridden mercantile system. We saw that Smith's attack on these arguments involved misrepresenting their purpose so that he could then treat them as failed attempts to achieve the purpose of his work – an analysis of wealth accumulation largely indifferent to security issues. The key dislocation here is that where counsel on trade treated questions of security and wealth simultaneously, Smith isolated wealth and was then forced to reintroduce security concerns at certain points. Uncoupled from geo-politics, Smith's analysis was unable to provide a stable basis for advice on what was formerly one of the constitutive concerns of counsel on trade.

We can use Smith's own words to summarize his position on this issue: to 'sacrifice the ordinary laws of justice to an idea of publick utility, to a sort of reasons of state' should only be excused 'in cases of the most urgent necessity'. Formerly, 'publick utility' had been the regular aim informing counsel, and therefore reason of state did not need to be invoked to justify deviation from some other regular yardstick, such as Smith's 'ordinary laws of justice' (Smith 1981 [1776]: Vol. I: 539). For a point of contrast, we can recall Mun's suggestion, that the notion that foreign trade should be protected because it supported the strength of the state was a 'Principal in Reason of State' (Mun 1928 [1664]: 88). In *Wealth of Nations*, trade was disengaged from reason of state, and less than one hundred years after Barbon complained that Machiavelli '*doth not mention* Trade, *as any way interested in the Affairs of State*' (Barbon 1690: Preface). At the same time, Smith treated reason of state as the reason that guided states only in exceptional circumstances, a precondition for the pejorative meaning it is typically given today. In this regard, Smith's counsel exhibited a certain academicism: the statesman was the addressee but his concrete needs were demoted in favour of conceptual sophistication. Correspondingly, Smith's attack on the mercantile system 'had distinct moral and political bearings' (Winch 1992: 100).[10]

The second peculiarity of Smith that needs to be underlined relates to the effects of his arguments, and here we revisit one of the guiding aims of our study: to chart the constitution of the international economy as a theoretical object. It is worth quoting again the key passage in which Smith projected the balance of produce and consumption onto an international context: the balance 'may take place in the whole globe of the earth, of which the wealth, population, and improvement may be either gradually increasing or gradually decaying' (Smith 1981 [1776]: Vol. I: 497).

This balance was the sum of the contributions made by individual nations, and it would likely be diminished by mercantile practices and fostered by a system of liberty. These assessments made it possible to evaluate a state's policy not for its effects on the strength and wealth of rivals, but on the world's wealth – the international economy. This was an object that the counsellor on trade could now cognize using arguments Smith had elaborated in *Wealth of Nations*, which offered new ways of construing trade and wealth in relation to the nations of the world.

It is true that Smith's forms of argument were primarily concerned with the government of wealth within a territory, and so the international economy was not at the centre of his analysis, but was rather an unintended side-effect of it. It follows that Smith's political œconomist was not an international economist, a figure specifically trained to theorize the international economy. (The history of this figure is not well known.) The key point for our narrative is that Smith's arguments separated wealth accumulation from power accumulation, and gave wealth over to its own logic, which had two modalities. One was static, in the sense that at a given point in time the world's capital would be allocated to its most profitable uses, which, in turn, directed labour within a nation. This allocation was a function of the self-love of agents, at least when their agency was not corrupted by circumstance or policy. The second modality was dynamic and embedded in historical time. This logic had capital move through the hierarchy of employments, starting with agriculture and ending with overseas trade, as nations moved through the successive stages of opulence. It was to this logic that the world's *telos* was attached, in the form of a collection of independent and opulent nations that regulated one another's conduct. It hardly needs pointing out that the partial equation CAPITAL + HISTORY has been completed in a variety of ways, each auguring a different future for the world. To this extent, we can construe these teleological projections as variations on a Smithian theme.[11]

We can finish this chapter by affirming the methodological stricture set out in the Introduction: not to treat the international economy as an object suddenly seized on by a consciousness freed from the tropes of power politics and imprecise concepts. By adopting our critical stance, we have instead been able to describe how the international economy came to be thought – through the operation of particular forms of argument that were first elaborated in the context of an intervention into the genre of counsel on trade in eighteenth-century Britain. The concept of the international economy did not reflect the trickle of globalization into everyday thinking, and nor did it mark the birth of an enlightened and cosmopolitan science: it was a second-order effect of shifts in practices of state counselling.

7 Ricardo and the national economy

Smith's *Wealth of Nations* represented a dislocation of the forms of argument that had previously typified counsel on trade. The most dramatic effect of the new arguments was the appearance of a new theoretical object, the international economy, which Smith's arguments made it possible to cognize. As we saw, however, Smith's arguments did not lead the counsellor to think of the national economy as an object distinct from the state, primarily for two reasons. The first was the unifying analytical figure of the statesman, who was invoked as the ordering agency that made laws regarding trade for the good of the polity. The second reason was the status of the moral agent described by Smith as the site of 'economic' decision-making, such as capital allocation. Smith's agent carried a form of subjectivity that held for all parts of life, and hence no economic subjectivity was theorized that could provide a basis for isolating economic activities from other types of activity. While Smith's arguments remained within 'the eighteenth-century science of politics' (Winch 1978: 187), they also separated the analysis of strength and wealth. Smith's crucial move was to equate wealth with labour, a category that was only relevant to state strength through the indirect channel of taxation.

Wealth of Nations enjoyed only modest influence in the decades following its first publication in 1776,[1] and significant elaborations of its central arguments largely had to wait until the nineteenth century. Crucially, Smith's portioning of strength and wealth was continued in this context, and one key moment of the nineteenth-century reception of Smith was James Mill's *Commerce Defended* (1965 [1808]). Mill formulated wealth in terms that were similar to Smith's annual produce, writing that a nation was poor or rich 'according as the quantity of property which she annually creates, in proportion to the number of her people, is great or is small' (ibid.: 105). This annual property was the product of a nation's different species of labour and, just like Smith, Mill privileged agricultural labour as the most productive source of wealth (ibid.: 13).[2] Another uptake of Smith in the nineteenth century was Robert Torrens's (1993 [1808]) *The Economists Refuted*. Torrens defined wealth as the stock of articles that fulfil wants and desires, and then nominated labour as the source of wealth: 'Labour creates wealth in three ways; by appropriating; by preparing; and by augmenting the productions of the land and water' (ibid.: 2).[3] These generalized conceptions of wealth enabled both Mill and Torrens to distinguish between different employments of capital, and they therefore operated an analysis of wealth that provided no direct entry point for the analysis of strength in the manner of eighteenth-century counsel on trade.

David Ricardo altered this reception context through his 1815 pamphlet, *An Essay on the Influence of a Low Price of Corn on the Profits of Stock* (Ricardo 2004 [1815]), and this text, along with his *On the Principles of Political Economy and Taxation* (Ricardo 2004 [1817]), will now occupy our attention. The focus on wealth to the exclusion of strength that Smith inaugurated was intensified in both these texts. Ricardo developed a conceptual apparatus to explain the relationship between three categories of wealth: profits, rent, and wages. Through these arguments Ricardo formulated a law of distribution that inversely related profits and rent, and hence the interests of landlords were opposed to capitalists and labourers. Ricardo therefore brings us to the second key moment in our overall narrative: the emergence of the economy as a sphere of activity that could be cognized as distinct from the state. Smith's statesman and his sympathetic moral subject were replaced by class interests grounded in a process of distribution. Our focus in what follows is the arguments that produced these effects.

Distribution and the national economy: *An Essay on the Influence of a Low Price of Corn on the Profits of Stock*

Ricardo's *Essay* was not his debut performance on matters of money and wealth, as he had already made important contributions to the Bullion Controversy of 1809–10. In that context, Ricardo developed arguments on the depreciation of the paper currency and the price of gold in relation to the circulation of precious metals, so that his analysis largely fitted into the contours of counsel on trade (Tribe 1978: 114–6). If we move forward to the *Essay*, however, we find Ricardo elaborating novel arguments in relation to the Corn Laws, which regulated the importation of wheat and other grains, referred to as corn.[4] In the *Essay*, Ricardo defined national wealth as the commodities that contributed to a nation's 'comforts and enjoyments' (Ricardo 2004 [1815]: 22), which was similar to Smith's notion of the annual produce. Unlike Smith, however, Ricardo offered little treatment of the sources of wealth in favour of examining the principles that regulated the rise and fall of rent and profits. This slide from wealth accumulation to distribution represented Ricardo's decisive point of innovation, and we turn to it now.

Ricardo's definition of rent was a central element of his theoretical structure. James Mill had conceived of rent as a surplus payment afforded by nature's productivity, and this distinguished agriculture from other trades. In other species of industry, Mill claimed, revenue provided for wages and profits, but in agriculture the return was sufficient for a rent payment to be made to the landlord (1965 [1808]: 13). Ricardo, by contrast, defined rent as the residual produce after the cost of production and the normal rate of profits had been deducted. Ricardo quoted Malthus's definition of rent approvingly:

> that portion of the value of the whole produce which remains to the owner, after all the outgoings belonging to its cultivation, of whatever kind, have

been paid, including the profits of the capital employed, estimated according to the usual and ordinary rate of the profits.

(Ricardo 2004a [1815]: 10)

Hence, rent was a residual – determined by the size of the two other shares in a given produce.

Ricardo proceeded to illustrate the implications of this point by examining the effects on rent and profits of cultivating progressively less desirable land. In a hypothetical original position, land ideally located was cultivated at a cost of 200 quarters of wheat, and it yielded a total produce of 300 quarters. Therefore, if rent was zero, there was a profit of 100 quarters, or 50 per cent. As population and wealth increased and more food was required, inferior lands were cultivated at an additional cost of 10 quarters. Profits on this second-rate land now fell to 90 quarters, or 43 per cent.

It was this cultivation of less desirable land and the consequent reduction in the size of the profit share that gave rise to rent. The mechanism at work here was the equalization of profits across all sectors. Ricardo mentioned Smith in an explanatory footnote, but his argument was not developed through an account of the self-loving agent but simply by the assertion that if profits were greater in trade than in agriculture, then 'capital would be withdrawn from the land to be employed in trade' (ibid.: 12). This process would continue until an approximate equality of profits was achieved.[5] In other words, and perhaps more intuitively: if the prevailing returns to capital were everywhere 43 per cent, the landlord of the first-rate land, where profits were 50 per cent, could extract rent of 7 per cent and leave the farmer in the same position as everyone else.

A further increase in population would increase the demand for food, drawing even less desirable land into cultivation, this time requiring capital of 220 quarters; consequently, profits on this land were 36 per cent. Rent on the first-rate land had now risen to 14 per cent (50 per cent minus 36 per cent), while second-rate land yielded rent for the first time of 7 per cent (43 per cent minus 36 per cent). With this third step in place, Ricardo could set out the *Essay*'s conceptual centrepiece:

> Thus by bringing successively land of a worse quality, or less favourably situated into cultivation, rent would rise on the land previously cultivated, and precisely in the same degree would profits fall; and if the smallness of profits do not check accumulation, there are hardly any limits to the rise of rent, and the fall of profit.
>
> (ibid.: 14)

Ricardo had identified an inexorable law, because even if landlords relinquished their rents, it would influence neither the price of corn nor the rate of profits: landlords relinquishing their rents would only 'enable those farmers, whose lands now pay a rent, to live like gentlemen' (ibid.: 22).

Identifying this law was an analytical achievement, but it came at a cost, for Ricardo was obliged to bracket the other determinants of the rate of profits. These were: first, the relative rates at which population and capital increased, second, improvements in the practice of agriculture, and third, the ability of foreign markets to supply cheap food (ibid.: 11–12, 25). Ricardo held these factors constant so that 'we may know what peculiar effects are to be ascribed to the growth of capital, the increase of population, and the extension of cultivation' (ibid.: 12). We can note here how Smith's historical and institutional analysis contrasted with Ricardo's highly specialized apparatus.

This specialization could be seen clearly in the *Essay* in regard to wealth, which did not enjoy the same intimate analytical connection with progress as it did in *Wealth of Nations*. For Smith, the natural march to opulence was accompanied by a shifting distribution of capital between competing employments, and these different uses were evaluated according to their contribution to the annual produce. The size of these contributions decreased as capital moved down the hierarchy of employments, starting with agriculture and ending with overseas trade. The Smithian schema therefore offered grounds to think that increasing levels of wealth would be accompanied by slowing rates of accumulation. This tendency could be temporarily disturbed by certain events, such as the discovery of new lands or the repeal of mercantile laws. Ultimately, however, progress represented a gradual brake on the accumulation of wealth, and indeed this was seen to be a distinguishing mark of western European nations. In Ricardo's *Essay*, progress implied the rise of population and a corresponding increase in the demand for food, which caused profits to fall and rents to rise. As a result, 'High rent and low profits ... ought never to be the subject of complaint, if they are the effect of the natural course of things. They are the most unequivocal proofs of wealth and prosperity' (ibid.: 21).

In line with Smith's account, Ricardo claimed that this general tendency towards rising rents and falling profits could be temporarily interrupted by the discovery of new markets that permitted the importation of cheap corn, and by improvements in agricultural technology (ibid.: 23). Despite this superficial similarity, at the point where historical time was brought into the analysis, there was a slide from wealth to rent and profits.

The related and more significant divergence between Smith's *Wealth of Nations* and Ricardo's *Essay* was the constitution of class interests. The landlords featured as Ricardo's parasitic class, enjoying a rent that was 'never a new creation of revenue, but always part of a revenue already created' (ibid.: 18). Tenant farmers represented the class that sustained the landlords under increasingly unfavourable conditions, whereas labourers stood as the industrious poor. Although Ricardo acknowledged that fluctuations in population would influence wages and therefore profits, this factor was suspended from the analysis at an early stage because 'nothing can be positively laid down' about the topic (ibid.: 23). As we will shortly see, Ricardo also read the relationship between profits and wages the other way around, by identifying the impact of profits on wages. He did this at key points to align the interests of labourers with those of farmers, and the interests of farmers were, by extension through the uniform rate of profits, the interests of capitalists in general. The interests of landlords were isolated as a minority interest due to these two links: between farmers and labourers, and between farmers and all capitalists.

Ricardo's system therefore made class conflict appear inevitable, because a landlord's interest was 'always opposed to the interest of every other class in the community' (ibid.: 21). The general increase in the difficulty of acquiring food served the landlord interest in two ways. On the one hand, inferior lands were cultivated, and this drove up rent. On the other hand, the price of corn normally increased at the same time as rent, so that a given quantity of rent could command a greater quantity of other goods for the landlord (ibid.: 20). As Winch has noted, this presentation foregrounded the 'passivity of rent as a form of income, if not its illegitimacy' (Winch 1996: 351).

By contrast, capitalists benefited from an increase in the rate of profits, and Ricardo identified three possible causes: a fall in wages, improvements in agriculture, and new markets that could supply cheap corn. The first two were not analytically tractable and the third was the *Essay*'s main quarry: cheap imported corn would increase the rate of profits (Ricardo 2004 [1815]: 25–6, 32–3). In brief, Ricardo's argument was that, in Britain, profits were kept low by the march of progress drawing inferior lands into cultivation. If corn raised on good lands overseas could be imported, then the capital employed on poor British lands could be diverted elsewhere more productively, most likely to produce goods that could be exchanged for the imported corn. Accordingly, the importation of corn would enable the normal process of rising rents and falling profits to be reversed.

Ricardo maintained that rising profits benefited the labourer. His comments on this point amounted to the claim that, as profits rose and more capital was accumulated, this

> would be beneficial to them [labourers], because the same capital would employ more hands; besides, that the greater profits would lead to further accumulation; and thus would a stimulus be given to population by really high wages, which could not fail for a long time to ameliorate the condition of the labouring classes.
>
> (ibid.: 35)

These arguments were not Ricardo's most convincing, and became less so when read alongside Chapter 5 of his *Principles*, 'On Wages', which we will do shortly. Nevertheless, these comments served to connect the interests of labour with capital. Having identified the component interests of society and divided them into a majority and a minority, Ricardo could proceed to recommend a policy on corn. He wrote that if 'the legislature were at once to adopt a decisive policy with regard to the trade in corn – if it were to allow a permanently free trade', then Britain would become an importing country. This was so because Britain's extensive wealth and population obliged it to apply capital to inferior lands to ensure its population's subsistence, when this capital would have been better directed to more profitable uses (ibid.: 26–7). The outcome of importing corn, as we have seen, would be to increase annual revenue, raise profits and reduce rents to the advantage of the majority of society. Ricardo used these arguments on the differential impact of freely importing corn to conclude his pamphlet with a stinging barb. It would be regretful, he wrote, if 'considerations for any particular class, are allowed to check the progress of the wealth and population of the country'. He continued his attack by writing that if the interests of landlords were so important as to disqualify his corn policy, then not only should importing corn be prohibited, but improving the implements of husbandry too, since this also reduced the price of corn and the landlord's rent (ibid.: 41).

We can now pause from our exposition to make a first sketch of the significance of Ricardo's arguments. The emergence of class interests grounded by distribution represented the most important break with *Wealth of Nations* and with the preceding forms of argument in counsel on trade. The class interests of landlords, capitalists, and workers were formed independently of moral accounts of the individual subject; neither were they legal or political entities. These classes derived their identity and status solely from an economic process, and this represented a crucial threshold for the formation of the national economy as an object of knowledge separate from the state (Tribe 1978: 127). Before developing this claim, two further points should be made to summarize the effects of the arguments Ricardo set out in the *Essay*. First, if we recall the way that Smith's statesman was required to weigh multiple considerations such as opulence and security, to apply general principles of political œconomy, and at times to depart from these principles, then in comparison Ricardo's 'legislature' was simply targeted as a law-making body that was urged to hear the voice of reason. The figure of the statesman (and his projected capacities) was not mobilized as a means of conceiving the organization of the polity and its government. Second, both the process through which wealth was accumulated, and the governmental practices by which this process was aided or impeded, were of secondary importance to the examination of distribution. Thus, from counsel on trade to Smith and then to Ricardo, strength was subjected to successive analytical displacements. This topic will be taken up in Chapter 8 in relation to foreign trade.

Distribution and the national economy: *On the Principles of Political Economy and Taxation*

The *Principles* did not represent a substantial break from the analysis of distribution contained in the *Essay*. It is true that, in the *Principles*, the value of a good was understood as a function of the total labour required to produce it, and Ricardo's elaboration of a labour theory of value was a result of his attempt to generalize the analysis he had presented in the *Essay* to include all commodities, not just corn.[6] Yet this shift between corn and labour as the device for representing value is not terribly significant from our point of view, for it did not alter the general effects of Ricardo's arguments nor did it shift his focus away from distribution. Nevertheless, by reviewing the extended treatment of certain themes in the *Principles*, we can make two embellishments to our account so far. The first is to more explicitly describe the laws that regulated wages and population, and the second is to draw out at greater length the relationship between the interests of labourers and the interests of capitalists, which was crucial to isolating landlords as a minority interest in society.

We saw above that Ricardo linked the interests of capitalists and labour indirectly, through capital accumulation. If we turn to Chapter 5 of the *Principles*, 'On Wages', we find Ricardo's discussion of the dynamics involved in this process. Ricardo opened this chapter by defining the natural price of labour as that which permitted labourers to 'subsist and to perpetuate their race, without either increase or diminution'. This price therefore depended on the cost of 'the quantity of food, necessaries, and conveniences' required to support a labourer and his family. Because food was a component part of the natural price of labour, labour was one of those rare commodities whose natural price rose with progress. In addition to changes in the price of labour owing to this cause, the market price of labour would normally move around its natural price simply from the vagaries of day-to-day exchange (Ricardo 2004 [1817]: 93). When the market price of labour rose above its natural price, the 'condition of the labourer is flourishing and happy', and the labouring population increased (ibid.: 94). An improving society was thus favourable to labourers because the accumulation of capital and resulting demand for labour could keep the market price of labour constantly above its natural price.

Different types of capital accumulation held different implications for the longevity of labour's happy condition. Capital typically consisted of clothes, food, tools, and machinery, and it may increase both in quantity and value at the same time (implying that, given Ricardo's labour theory of value, proportionally more labour was required to produce the capital increment). But if the increase in capital was an effect of new machinery, then there may be no increase in the proportional quantity of labour required to produce this capital. Here, the *value* of the two different quantities of capital would be the same (through the operation of the labour theory of value). In the first case, the natural price of labour would rise (because the cost of producing subsistence had risen), but in the second case it would not. Correspondingly, although the increase in absolute labour used would raise the market price of labour in both cases, the labourer's position was superior in the second case, as the cost of subsistence had not increased with wages (ibid.: 95–6). Or, to use contemporary language, real wages would be higher in the second case.

On the basis of this analysis, it seems that the interests of labourers were aligned with the expansion of machinery in production. Ricardo's revision of this position will be considered shortly. The concluding point to take from this discussion is that while real wage increases would be higher or lower depending on the type of capital accumulation, in either case they could be treated as temporary because they triggered population growth in the labouring class, which acted to align the market price of labour with its natural price (ibid.: 97). These multiple determinations of wages were then overlaid with an account of progress. In new settlements with abundant fertile land, capital accumulated faster than labour could reproduce itself. In such cases, the 'power of production is still greater than that of population', and this placed upwards pressure on wages. Such increase, we are told, would 'not long continue so', because the quality of land would decline with the spread of cultivation even as 'the power of population continues always the same'. The relationship between population and wages would then be reversed: population would place downward pressure on wages until they reached the subsistence point, and at this point wages would begin to exert pressure on population (ibid.: 98–9).

In addition to a diminishing supply of land, progress was also manifested as the cultivation of refined tastes by the labouring class. The effect of labour acquiring such tastes was to raise the natural price of labour, which could then act as a 'refuge from calamity', since a fall below a subsistence wage that included luxuries would check the growth of population through taste for comfort instead of abject poverty. It followed that 'friends of humanity cannot but wish that in all countries the labouring classes should have a taste for comforts and enjoyments' and, moreover, they 'should be stimulated by all legal means in their exertions to procure them' (ibid.: 100–1). Counsel on trade typically conceived of luxury as enervating the strength of the state and the virtue of the people, but in Ricardo's hands luxury performed a humanitarian role. Another strand will be added to the story of luxury shortly. While the rise of refinement was a friend to the labourer, he was still beset by the general tendency for the price of food to increase. Mounting food costs did cause wages to grow, but it was generally insufficient to compensate for the increased costs of other commodities occasioned by the rising cost of food. In other words, if workers were to cultivate refined tastes, they required a disposable income after purchasing food; but according to Ricardo, in the normal course of progress the size of the worker's disposable income was eroded gradually (ibid.: 101–4).

Having set down the laws that regulated wages, Ricardo claimed that they were well executed by the 'fair and free competition of the market', but the market had been impeded by the legislature. Ricardo took aim at the Poor Laws: 'The clear and direct tendency of the poor laws, is in direct opposition to these obvious principles.' In order to demonstrate the mistaken ideas that had recently predominated, Ricardo quoted from a 1796 parliamentary address by William Pitt, in which Pitt argued that the laws represented due assistance for those who had increased the national population. Ricardo maintained that, luckily for England, the increase in population that the system of support to the poor had engendered was what the period of 'progressive prosperity' would have called forth naturally in the absence of the laws. This fortunate arrangement had hitherto protected society, but the 'principle of gravitation is not more certain than the tendency of such laws to change wealth and power into misery and weakness' (ibid.: 105–8; 107 at ∗). For Ricardo, nothing less than the eventual abolition of the offending laws would suffice.

Such was Ricardo's position on wages and population. We can now turn to the second detail to be gleaned from the *Principles*: the link between the interests of labour and capital. In the *Essay*, this link was established by claiming that increased profits allowed capital accumulation, which in turn set more labour to work. This link was maintained in the *Principles*, but its veracity was called into question by the variable presentation of the role of machinery. On the one hand, the interests of labour could be aligned with the introduction of new machinery when this raised real wages by increasing the quantity but not the value of subsistence goods, as we have just noted. On the other hand, in Chapter 6, 'On Profits', Ricardo developed arguments that challenged this presumption.

Ricardo started the chapter by describing the general relationship between profits and wages. We have seen that the last unit of land cultivated did not yield rent, and that no rent was paid in manufactures, so that in both cases revenue was only divided between profits and wages. As the price of corn increased from the expansion of cultivation, the natural price of labour rose too, and this decreased the size of the residual share for profits. A declining rate of profits was accordingly both a sign of progress and a check upon it, because

> the farmer and manufacturer can no more live without profit, than the labourer without wages. Their motive for accumulation will diminish with every diminution of profit, and will cease altogether when their profits are so low as not to afford them an adequate compensation for their trouble.
>
> (ibid.: 122)

Happily, though, the decline of profits could be slowed by 'improvements in machinery, connected with the production of necessaries, as well as by discoveries in the science of agriculture which enable us to relinquish a portion of labour before required' (ibid.: 120). Machinery could reduce the wages of labour by reducing the labour content of the goods on which labourers subsisted, and this protected the size of the profit share.

Taking together the points made so far, we must conclude that machinery occupied an ambiguous position with respect to labour's interests: it could increase the real wages of labour, it could prolong accumulation and therefore the expansion of work, but it could also result in a contraction of labour employed. In the third edition of the *Principles*, published in 1821, Ricardo added a new chapter, 'On Machinery'. The stated purpose of the new chapter was to examine 'the influence of machinery on the interests of the different classes of society' (ibid.: 386). Ricardo wrote that his former views regarding labour derived from the belief that, even if the introduction of machinery resulted in a diminished demand for labour in relation to one task, there was every reason to expect that both the retrenched labour and the capital that had previously set it to work would simply be reallocated. This belief was rejected in the new chapter. While both landlord and capitalist were seen to benefit from the introduction of machinery, in general, it was 'very injurious to the interests of the class of labourers' (ibid.: 388).

Ricardo's reconsideration relied on a distinction between gross and net income. Gross income was the fund that supplied both the necessaries of labour and the capitalist's profit, while net income referred to the profit portion of this fund only. The interests of the capitalist lay with the size of net income (with profits) and labour's with gross income (with subsistence). Accordingly, if a portion of capital was transferred from the production of gross income to the purchase of machinery, with no effect on profits, the capitalist's interest would be unaffected, while labour's would be directly harmed (ibid.: 388–9). In sum, the 'discovery and use of machinery may be attended with a diminution of gross produce', and when this occurred 'it will be injurious to the labouring class' (ibid.: 390). Put differently, there was a difference between fixed and circulating capital from the point of view of labour. On the other hand, the introduction of machinery could also spur accumulation in the ways suggested above, in which case this negative effect could be mitigated, and even completely overturned. In addition, the notion that the state might discourage the use of machinery was decried as the road to wrack and ruin, for if 'capital is not allowed to get the greatest net revenue that the use of machinery will afford here, it will be carried abroad' (ibid.: 396). Ricardo thus hedged his analysis.

After providing his concluding comments on the relationship between the introduction of machinery and the interests of labourers, Ricardo offered a few points on the implications of how net income was spent, and quickly noting his comments will allow us to return to one of the minor threads of our story, the status of luxury goods. Ricardo claimed that the labouring class had 'no small interest in the manner in which the net income of the country is expended'. If, for example, a landlord were to spend his revenue 'in the manner of an ancient baron, in the support of a great number of retainers, or menial servants', then more labour would be employed than if that revenue were spent on 'fine clothes, or costly furniture . . . or in the purchase of any other luxuries' (ibid.: 392–3). Earlier in this chapter we described the role of luxuries in cushioning labour from calamity when wages fell, but here it featured as a missed opportunity to support the employment of labour. Both treatments examined luxuries from the point of view of labour as a distinct class, and this points us to what has changed in the history of luxury. First, in Ricardo's work the status of luxuries as an object of moral anxiety and threat to state security had been eroded by an analysis that examined luxuries from the point of view of the distribution of wealth. Second, Ricardo's conclusion that menial servants were a better allocation of income than luxury goods (from the point of view of labour) partially reversed Smith's treatment, which represented servants as unproductive labour.

The divergence between Smith and Ricardo over luxury was symptomatic of the analytical movement embodied in Ricardo's work, and this in turn directs us to the formation of the economy as a distinct domain with a specialized mode of analysis. This analysis was not concerned with state strength but with the allocation of rents, profits, and wages. In Ricardo's words, to 'determine the laws which regulate this distribution, is the principal problem in Political Economy'. He continued by reflecting on his forebears, 'much as the science has been improved by the writings of Turgot, Stuart, Smith, Say, Sismondi, and others', these authors nevertheless afforded 'very little satisfactory information respecting the natural course of rent, profit, and wages' (ibid.: 5). Political economy's emphasis on distribution, which Ricardo acknowledged in his comments, did not divert the Smithian stream but rather dammed it up, by shifting attention from the state (and wealth accumulation) to the economy (and wealth distribution). This marks the resting point for our history of the national economy as a theoretical object.

Conclusion

The political economist who had mastered the arguments set out in Ricardo's texts would conceive of national wealth as being distributed between three classes via the inverse relationship between profits and rent, and the determination of wages by the interaction of population and capital accumulation dynamics. This distribution occurred in a conceptual space populated by classes whose existence was grounded solely by the discursive instruments that projected this space – the Ricardian analysis of distribution. That is, and as we noted in relation to the *Essay*, these classes were not treated as bearing legal or moral status. Instead, Ricardo's classes were defined by their position in relations of distribution – receiving a share in the nation's wealth that was subjected to certain economic processes. This sphere of activity was therefore independent of the state, in terms of the subjects it was populated by and the arguments that made it cognizable. The possibility for the political economist to accede to these relations of distribution was a consequence of Ricardo's raising the level of abstraction at which a recurring issue – the Corn Laws – was debated. The practical means for this act of abstraction was constructing rent and profits as theoretically defined categories in a determined relation to one another. In other words, the key development was to treat rent as a residual inversely related to the rate of profits. Emphasizing the level of abstraction is a crucial sub-requirement of our critical approach to the economy, for it allows us to note that economic argument has operated at different levels of abstraction and with different effects, one of which was to make the economy thinkable in the sense we have been concerned with throughout our account – as a domain separate from the state.

The key element here is the emergence of distinct class interests that were determined by relations of production and distribution. To draw out this point more fully, we can notice Smith's comments on the major classes in society and their interests, which at first blush appear to be similar to the classes Ricardo described. Smith maintained that a nation's annual produce was divided between rent, wages, and profit, and that each share corresponded with one of the three 'great, original and constituent orders' of society: landlords, labourers, and merchants and manufacturers. In terms of objective interests, landlords were well suited to policy-making because every improvement of society raised their class's rent receipts, which Smith treated as a monopoly payment that the landlord did his best to maximize, subject to 'what the farmer can afford to give'.[7] Alas, the landlord's comfortable situation made him indolent, which in turn made him ignorant and even incapable of applying his mind to consider the consequences of this or that proposed trade regulation. The land proprietor should therefore not always be trusted to know his own interest best (Smith 1981 [1776]: Vol. I: 161, 265). In Ricardo's analysis, the landlord's interests were opposed to society's by definition, through the inverse relationship between profits and rent. Furthermore, there was no reintegration of the landlord class into state and society through the contextual description of moral agency after the Smithian fashion. Put differently, the political economist who had mastered Ricardo's arguments did not need to engage in such descriptions of moral agency to understand class interests because these interests could be derived from the analysis of distribution.

Our critical approach to the economy also leads us to notice the differing ways in which economic argument has been inserted into practices of government. Ricardo imagined the link between his analysis and legislation in relatively mechanistic terms. Far from Smith's statesman, who may, for example, judge that a policy of unfettered international trade should be temporarily set aside in the name of humanity, Ricardo primarily conceived of the role of political economy as elaborating scientific knowledge that was then absorbed by Parliament. Consider this statement in a letter to Say in 1820:

> Political economy is making progress in this country. Every day correct principles advance… The proceedings in parliament last sessions gave great satisfaction to the friends of the science. The true principles of currency were at length solemnly recognized; and I should hope that we never again can go astray.
>
> (Ricardo 2004 [1819–21]: 150)

Ricardo's work as a politician in Parliament, starting from 1819, was the corollary to this conception of knowledge transmission. His pamphlet, *On Protection to Agriculture*, was published in April 1822, just a few days before the Report of the Agricultural Committee was due to be debated, and new editions were called for within days of the pamphlet's first publication (Sraffa 2004a: 3–5). Few macroeconomists today can claim such direct influence on the minds of legislators, so we should not take abstraction to mean distance from policy-making. Nevertheless, it was the act of abstraction embodied in Ricardo's arguments that separated state and economy.

One of the consequences of this separation was the untying of the analytical torsion in counsel on trade that we described in Chapter 3. This torsion arose between the fiscal-military state's need to extract money, men, and bullion from the state's circulation to provide for its own strength, and representations of circulation as a self-directing process that would be harmed by such actions. To focus on men, recall that population was a key concern for counsel on trade, which was understood as the sum of men in different trades, who were of greater or lesser importance to the state as sources of strength and wealth depending on the characteristics of their trade. Hume thus treated manufacturing as valuable because it acted as a store of labour that could be conscripted by the state. Ricardo treated population as a phenomenon that possessed its own rhythms – advancing and receding at a quicker or slower pace than capital depending on circumstances. We can thus note the general appropriateness of Foucault's characterization of population as a complex datum. The significant point that leads us to refine Foucault's account is that, contrary to his presentation, the torsion that typified counsel on trade was not dissolved because sovereignty was disqualified as a model for the government of trade. Rather, political economy centred the question of the relationship between profits and rent instead of the state's strength and wealth. The image of intellectual change that we should hold is therefore one of forms of argument emerging and receding, rather than the successive outmoding of political technologies.

8 Ricardo and the international economy

Attention now turns to Ricardo's treatment of international trade, and our task is to inquire after the object that the political economist who had mastered Ricardo's arguments was led to cognize. We have seen in Chapter 6 that the political œconomist who mobilized Smith's arguments regarding the allocation of capital and trade between nations could analyse the dynamics that governed the accumulation of the world's wealth and describe the inhibiting effects of state actions. Ricardo's arguments diverged significantly from Smith's in relation to national wealth, in particular by focusing on distribution and largely sidelining issues relating to wealth accumulation. This analytical demotion of wealth accumulation in the national context was repeated in relation to international trade, for Ricardo's arguments concentrated on the implications of trade for the rate of profits. In tandem, Smith's relative silence on questions of strength and security was intensified in Ricardo's work, resulting in a benign portrait of international relations that was most famously expressed in the notion of comparative advantage. Our account will begin by returning to the arguments of the *Essay*.

International trade

The general argumentative thrust of the *Essay* was that the majority interest in society would gain from a free corn trade. The essential idea was that if cheap corn were imported, capital engaged in cultivating low-quality land could be freed and applied to more productive projects, and this would raise profits and lower rents, along with causing food prices to fall. Ricardo maintained that in view of these benefits, it was untenable to allow the interests of a single class to stand in the way of the free importation of corn. This was an economic argument, in the sense that the material welfare of society provided the basis for appraising policy. In the *Essay*, Ricardo also countenanced the security argument that dependence on external sources for a significant portion of the food supply was dangerous. He claimed that given the significant material costs of failing to pursue a free trade policy, the arguments from security would need to be 'almost unanswerable' to justify such a position (Ricardo 2004 [1815]: 26). We are told that neither of the two arguments typically advanced in this context were unanswerable, as we shall now see.

The first line of defence for preserving restrictions on imports of corn asserted that dependence on other nations for food was unacceptable. The animating fear was that a combination of continental powers could interrupt the supply of food during wartime. Ricardo flatly rejected this argument as implausible in view of the likely effects of free trade and the practical realities of trading relationships between states. First, Britain's high levels of wealth and population had forced it to cultivate inferior lands to supply its corn needs. A free trade would therefore allow Britain to import large quantities of corn and draw capital off these low-quality lands for more efficient use elsewhere. Second, it was misguided to imagine that the nations who had thus become accustomed to supplying Britain would then suddenly prohibit exports, since this would cause 'ruinous commercial distress' to those who had committed capital to supplying the British market. No sovereign would willingly impose such distress on his people, but even if such a measure were attempted, the people would certainly throw off such a heavy yoke. Third, a concerted effort to interrupt Britain's imports 'could not come upon us suddenly', and Ricardo argued that Britain would have sufficient time to respond by bringing low-quality lands into cultivation again, or by securing a supply from states not involved in the conflict (ibid.: 28–9).

The second argument against imports was essentially Malthus's fear that in bad seasons, when supplies of corn were limited, the exporting nation would privilege its own population at the expense of Britain's. According to Ricardo, Malthus had omitted to notice that Britain's demand would encourage the exporting countries to greatly expand their agricultural production. The other factor that discounted the danger was the tendency for bad harvests to be matched by good harvests in another part of the same nation or in foreign nations. Consequently, overall supply rarely fluctuated in the way required by Malthus's argument (ibid.: 28–31).

A point of keen interest in these arguments is the way Ricardo related security issues to his foregoing narrative. Ricardo shifted his discussion from the distributive effects of importing cheap corn to the potential security consequences by posing a rhetorical question: would it be wise to legislate 'with the view of preventing an evil which might never occur; and to ward off a most improbable danger, sacrifice annually a revenue of some millions?' Unlike Smith's exceptions to a policy of free trade, which offered the statesman pointers to a valid casuistry premised on the existence of branches of legislative science beyond political œconomy, Ricardo's comments were purely offensive in character. He portrayed the dangers of international politics as ephemeral – they 'might never occur' – and described arguments based on such dangers as 'matters of opinion'. In contrast, the economic losses that arose from a protectionist policy driven by phantasmic fears could 'be reduced to accurate calculation' (ibid.: 27, 29–30).

If we look back to pre-Smithian counsel on trade, we see that international security was at the centre of analysis, automatically justifying the adjustment of trade practices and alliances. In the terms of Ricardo's analysis, however, security concerns were made to appear vague and ill-defined next to the clear material gains offered by a policy of free trade. In short, the breach between questions of strength and the analysis of wealth that Smith had introduced was widened by Ricardo's arguments.

Distribution and the international economy

We now turn to the arguments Ricardo set out on international trade in the *Principles*, and here we encounter his distinction between wealth (the quantity of commodities) and value (labour). A nation's annual labour was taken as fixed, but the quantity of foreign commodities that this labour could be exchanged for varied. It followed that foreign trade did not raise the amount of value in a nation, but only the mass of commodities. For example, if an English merchant purchased a quantity of Portuguese wine for £1000 and sold it for £1200, then it was of no consequence to the merchant if the quantity of wine was 25 cases or 50, because in either situation his profits were 20 per cent, and £1000 was the value of English goods with which he parted. On the other hand, the wealth of England was clearly greater when it consisted of 50 cases of wine instead of 25 (Ricardo 2004 [1817]: 128).

Ricardo used this distinction between wealth and value to deny Smith's claim that, when a new overseas trade yielded profits above the prevailing rate, profit equalization would occur through a rise in the general rate of profits. In *Wealth of Nations*, Smith's equalizing mechanism was the higher rate of profits drawing capital from existing trades, so that competition increased in the new trade (causing profits to fall), and decreased in the old trades (causing profits to rise), until parity was achieved (Smith 1981 [1776]: Vol. I: 110). Ricardo maintained instead that while profits would harmonize, this did not occur through profits rising in the old trades. The difference turned on Ricardo's treatment of value as a fixed stock, a portion of which was traded in exchange for foreign goods. Ricardo asserted, in a rather unhelpful way, that this traded portion could either rise or fall. If the portion fell, then there would be more available value to buoy the demand for domestic produce, in which case capital would not be diverted from the old trades. If the portion rose, however, demand for the produce of the old trades would have decreased, and no stimulus to prices and profits would have resulted (Ricardo 2004 [1817]: 129–31). In either case, Ricardo showed that the Smithian view – that profits rose in the old trades – was flawed.

Our presentation of Ricardo's arguments is abbreviated and simplified because their recondite details are less important for our purposes than their function in the overall argument, which was to allow Ricardo to restate his familiar refrain: profits could only be affected by a change in wages. The relevance of overseas trade to profit determination therefore lay in its ability to bring the necessaries of labour – such as corn and clothes – to market at reduced prices (ibid.: 132). Ricardo described foreign trade as 'highly beneficial to a country' because it increased the 'abundance and cheapness of commodities'; nevertheless, foreign trade engendered 'no tendency to raise the profits of stock', except when the commodities imported were those 'on which the wages of labour are expended' (ibid.: 133). In comparing Smith's and Ricardo's formulations of trade between nations, the most significant point of difference was that Ricardo's analysis was geared towards questions of distribution, rather than the effects of trade on wealth accumulation. In *Wealth of Nations*, accumulation was conceived of as capital setting productive labour to work, and the central issues were the quantity of labour, the country to which this labour belonged, and how often the capital returned home in a year. For Ricardo, on the other hand, trade was primarily treated from the perspective of profits.

A similar conclusion emerges when we compare the role of teleology and capital accumulation in *Wealth of Nations* and the *Principles*. Like Smith, Ricardo developed his discussion of capital accumulation in conjunction with a typology of nations, which we previewed in Chapter 7. In one type of country, the 'new settlements', arts and knowledge could be introduced by advanced nations and, given that good land was available, capital would initially increase at a faster rate than population. This tendency would ultimately be arrested by the mechanism of decreasing profits, the inevitable result of the fact that land was finite and of different grades. That is, every increase of capital employed on the land yielded a 'decreased rate of production, whilst the power of population continues always the same' (ibid.: 98). A second type of nation was a territory abundant in fertile land but largely uncultivated due to the 'ignorance, indolence, and barbarism of the inhabitants'. In this case, the population was constantly subjected to want and privation, which would check population growth. The scarcity of fertile land was therefore not the issue for this second category of nation. Rather, what was required was for the people to be 'better governed and instructed', especially in relation to security of property and good government. So transformed, nations of this type would begin the process of improvement, effectively joining the first type of nation on its march towards the stationary state brought on by the finite supply of land and lowness of profits. In the last type of nation there was no need for improvement because the land was already highly cultivated; in fact, if capital accumulation continued, it would only exacerbate the clash between population and food supply (ibid.: 99).

Recall that Smith treated colonies as places that advanced rapidly in wealth, and for two key reasons. First, colonies could follow the optimal development path and devote the largest share of their capital to agriculture. Second, colonies could also avoid certain institutional handicaps, such as primogeniture, which slowed the process of accumulation. Ricardo glossed Smith's account of the institutional aspect of development in a few sentences, and presented his doctrine of diminishing returns in agriculture in place of Smith's analysis of capital allocation. In short, the Smithian treatment of wealth accumulation and the institutions of government gave way in Ricardo to examining the factors that regulated distribution. We can construe this shift in attention as a consequence of the specialization embodied in Ricardo's conceptual apparatus.

The focus on distribution was also on display in Ricardo's other category for conceiving of nations – as relatively fertile or infertile, which influenced how quickly profits tended to zero. This rate was given by two factors: first, and most importantly, the extent of fertile land; and, second, whether the importation of corn was prohibited. In nations with ample fertile land, the extension of cultivation would raise rents and decrease profits at a slower rate than in a nation where fertile land was scarce, because the need to cultivate inferior lands would be delayed. Regarding the second factor, importing corn, if a nation had reached the point at which importing corn was profitable and such importation was permitted, then profits would be buoyed by the downward pressure on wages and the diminished need to extend cultivation to inferior lands (ibid.: 126).

We can now examine these two typologies side by side. In Chapter 6, Smith's categorization of nations was seen to have an administrative-scientific character, which contrasted with the diplomatic-military nature typical of earlier counsel on trade. Like Smith, Ricardo developed an analysis that was removed from international power politics. But further, Ricardo's categories were thoroughly developmental in character because they apprehended nations in terms of their distance from the stationary state, and how quickly scanty profits would begin to act as an anchor on accumulation. Hence, the condition of inter-state rivalry that a counsellor on trade typically described was not an object that the Ricardian political economist was led to conceive of through his study of distribution. In the first place, the political economist apportioned shares of wealth rather than power. In addition, the political economist was concerned with speeds of progress, so that the size of wealth shares changed through time. In Chapter 2, we noted Bolingbroke's description of change in world politics as both the effect of great events – such as the destruction of governments – and as the outcome of a series of gradual shifts. Bolingbroke's redistributions of power were not inscribed in historical patterns of progress that the counsellor was intended to theorize; change was simply what appeared to happen from the perspective of a statesman's hindsight.[1] We might therefore hazard to suggest that one of the distinguishing features of the Ricardian political economist was the ability to cognize processes of economic development in terms of rates of growth and the onset of the stationary state.

To now consider comparative advantage, we find Ricardo turning to this well-known aspect of his analysis in the context of discussing the effect of foreign trade on profits.[2] As the immediate preamble, Ricardo reminded the reader that foreign trade could increase the mass of commodities to be enjoyed but not the profits of stock, unless the imported commodities were those required by labourers to subsist. This lesson was then repeated in relation to domestic trade, and so we learn that neither the distribution nor the division of labour affected profits, and here we see Smithian themes demoted again. Ricardo then considered relative value across countries. His essential claim was that different forces regulated profits in each country. A profit differential within England, say, between London and Yorkshire, would be equalized by capital shifting between the two cities. But this process did not operate between nations. Ricardo developed his claim by imagining Portugal as a closed economy that was obliged to produce both wine and cloth for itself. The quantity of wine that Portugal would be prepared to give for English cloth was not determined by the costs of producing cloth in Portugal in the way that we might expect. Ricardo illustrated his point with a numerical example that had Portugal making wine with the labour of 80 men, and cloth with the labour of 90, whereas

England made cloth with the labour of 100 men and wine for the effort of 120. Hence, inside the Portuguese economy, it cost more to make cloth (90 versus 80). But if cloth was acquired from England in exchange for wine, then the cost for Portugal would only be 80 – the cost of the wine given to England expressed in terms of Portuguese labour. The fact that Portugal had an absolute cost advantage in both goods over England (80 and 90 versus 120 and 100) was irrelevant, for Portugal only consulted its own comparative costs. In this case, the immediate gain would be the labour of 10 men (90 minus 80) (ibid.: 133–5).[3]

This was the difference between trade within a nation and trade across nations: the 'labour of 100 Englishmen cannot be given for that of 80 Englishmen, but the produce of the labour of 100 Englishmen may be given for the produce of the labour of 80 Portuguese'. English capitalists and consumers in both countries would clearly benefit if cloth and wine were produced solely in Portugal, which would require England's capital and cloth-making labour to migrate to Portugal. Then profits and the natural price of wine and cloth would be regulated as if between London and Yorkshire, where only transport costs stood in the way of profit equalization. Since such capital flight did not occur, free trade did not threaten the nation with economic dissolution. The proximate cause for the divergence in relative values between the two countries – which resulted in the persistence of national borders – was the reluctance with which capital was moved from one country to another. This reluctance owed to the 'fancied or real insecurity of capital, when not under the immediate control of its owner', and the 'natural disinclination which every man has to quit the country of his birth and connexions' (ibid.: 135–6).

The interesting point to notice in Ricardo's argument is that the flight of capital was inhibited by the desire for security, which was equated with supervision. This was the substance of Smith's account of why, given similar rates of profit, capital would be allocated to domestic industry over foreign industry. This preference for security played no small part in Smith's system: it explained why the private pursuit of gain was aligned naturally with the public interest, as though by an 'invisible hand'. That is, Smith needed the security motive to undergird the desirability of his system of liberty from the perspective of the statesman. Ricardo enlisted the preference for security to a different but no less vital purpose – ensuring the existence of the nation state as an economic unit. More explicitly, Ricardo coupled the security motive with national sentiment to explain why the world economy was characterized by trade between nations based on comparative costs, such as England and Portugal. Without this prop, we might imagine, trade would lead to a post-state world of trading locations distinguished only by transport costs, like cities in a state, in the manner of London and Yorkshire.

Conclusion

Ricardo's treatment of international trade mirrored his analysis of domestic production by placing the question of distribution at the centre of inquiry. This had several implications for how the Ricardian political economist would conceive of the international economy. The first was that the Ricardian framework was developmental in character: it placed nations onto economic growth paths that were ultimately governed by the fact of diminishing returns in agriculture. The key discursive mechanism here was Ricardo's raising the level of abstraction at which the categories of rent and profit were connected in theoretical argument. As we saw in Chapter 7, raising the level of abstraction in relation to domestic production resulted in isolating the economy as a self-regulating domain. One of the flow-on effects at the international level was that economic development was construed primarily in terms of a projected clash between the population and the food supply, and the work of the Ricardian political economist was to describe the manner of its approach.

A second effect of Ricardo's analysis was to lead the political economist to abstract away from multiple causal factors in order to trace out the effects of selected variables one at a time. In relation to comparative advantage, for example, Ricardo acknowledged that his analysis was based on the simplifying assumption of two nations and two commodities. Ultimately, however, there were additional factors at play (the role of money, improvements in arts and machinery, bounties, and taxes), which were 'constantly operating on the natural course of trade' (ibid.: 141). Smith's balance of produce and consumption, on the other hand, represented a unifying analytic with which to conceive of the operation of the international economy. The Smithian political œconomist therefore faced a smaller analytical burden than their Ricardian successor. The corresponding difference was the mode of address: Smith's counsel to the statesman required the political œconomist to set out general principles and relevant exceptions that could form the basis of a legislator's reasoning when making laws to regulate trade. In this respect, Ricardo's task was comparatively ambitious because he was attempting to determine the laws that regulated distribution for nations engaging in foreign trade and existing in historical time. Ricardo's framework was not intended to provide a basis for reasoning and argument, but to constitute the actual argument; thus, he felt Malthus was wrong to think that political economy was not 'a strict science like the mathematics' (Ricardo 2004 [1819–21]: 331).[4] Viewed in terms of the intellectual labour required of the political economist, the fact of Ricardo's theoretical sophistication was as understandable as his inconsistencies and analytical tautologies.[5]

A final point needs to be made in regard to the radical ontology that accompanied Ricardo's international economy. In particular, the security motive – which explained why capital was retained for domestic production rather than migrating overseas – seems to give only tenuous protection to a nation's capital. The profit/security trade-off would presumably have become untenable in the presence of sufficiently high rates of profit, so that capital would indeed have been removed from one nation to another in search of superior returns. The other factor maintaining the borders of the nation state was cultural attachment. Together, then, capital security and culture held the nation's borders in place. Yet the effect of the nation state as a political form was to inhibit the expansion of material plenty in the world – because national borders were non-economic in nature. Thus, Ricardo's arguments made it possible to cognize the international economy as a collection of nations that acted as containers of capital and labour, and these nations then traded with one another on the basis of cost differences. International power politics had become unhinged from the analysis of trade, or, perhaps more appropriately, political economy had emerged not only as a science of wealth with little to say about power, but as one that could look dubiously at the very existence of the nation state.

9 Conclusion

We began this book by promising to provide a critical history of the national economy and the international economy, and by claiming that its distinguishing feature would be a self-conscious refusal of bi-level approaches to history that split economic ideas and economic reality. This commitment directed our inquiry away from presuming the progress of economic science in the traditional way – as a body of knowledge that captures the nature of the economy with increasing accuracy. We also relinquished the presumption that the economy is a naturally given object that simply exists in the world. In place of these assumptions, and drawing on the work of Michel Foucault, Keith Tribe, and contextual historiography, our account was guided by the notion of forms of argument as a means to treat economic theorizing as an activity that could be described in an historical manner. The two essential steps were, first, to examine how authors writing on trade and money in the early modern period constructed their arguments and, second, to determine the objects of knowledge that were cognized using these arguments. One of the crucial consequences of adopting this approach was that we could examine how some arguments made it possible to think of the economy as a domain independent and distinct from the state, and how some arguments did not lead to such a conceptualization.

The portrait that we produced was consequently not one of early economists groping towards contemporary economic doctrine in the half-light of their limiting historical circumstances. Instead, we described how counsellors to statesmen presupposed the state as the target of their counsel, and thought of trade as one of the state's modalities of power. The state these counsellors presupposed was treated as both the site and agent of administration, and the administrative programmes they recommended were seen as necessary to the survival of the state in a world of threatening rivalries. In particular, states competed in terms of strength and wealth to achieve universal monarchy, or fought to keep this prospect at bay. One of the key elements of this intellectual context was that strength and wealth were intimately related categories, and this accounted for much of the bad reputation usually attached to so-called mercantilist thought. In fact, we saw that the 'mercantile system' was a retrospective rhetorical creation deployed to great effect by Adam Smith when reconstructing counsel on trade as a foil to his own arguments. While Smith's *Wealth of Nations* was still an example of counsel on trade, it nevertheless altered some of the genre's structuring forms of argument.

Three of Smith's innovations were especially important. The first was to replace the complex analysis of interdigitation between strength and wealth by defining wealth in terms of an independent and homogeneous category – labour. The second was the partial eclipse of the statesman as the polity's organizing figure by the actions of self-directing moral agents. The third change was an effect of the first two: Smith raised the level of abstraction at which arguments regarding trade and wealth operated. As a consequence of this act of abstraction, Smith could elaborate a sophisticated analysis of capital allocation that had unprecedented effects in counsel on trade. In fact, this made it possible for the Smithian political œconomist to accede to the international economy as an object distinct from the actions of states. This was the first major step towards our critical history, for we could show that conceiving of an international economy was not the result of amateur economists clearing away misty notions and perceiving the nature of the world as it really was for the first time. Rather, understood as a specific intellectual object, the international economy was an effect of Smith's new forms of argument. These arguments split the analysis of strength from wealth and made it possible to look askance at the actions of states that had a negative impact on capital allocation, and hence on the world's accumulation of wealth. In relation to the national economy, however, Smith's arguments did not delineate the economy as a separate field from the province of state action. His arguments related to state administration, of which trade was just one aspect; further, in the Smithian system capital was allocated by moral – rather than economic – agents. Yet Smith's arguments played a vital role in the emergence of the economy as a distinct domain by separating the analysis of wealth from the analysis of strength, for this was a practice that Ricardo inherited and extended.

Our account of Ricardo's challenging work focused on the centrality of distribution to his analysis, which posited three economic classes that were grounded not by moral or legal arguments, but by the relations between rent, profits, and wages. We claimed that by raising the level of abstraction at which arguments relating profits and rent operated, Ricardo's analysis of distribution made it possible to think of the economy as a domain separate from the state. The essential point was that the relations between Ricardo's categories were self-sustaining as a consequence of having been abstracted away from the terrain of state administration. A further result of this abstraction was the statesman's displacement as a means of imagining the nature of economic government, thereby cancelling a crucial feature of both counsel on trade and Smithian political œconomy. The humanistic image of counsel offered by a subject to a sovereign was replaced by the imperative to disseminate the scientific insights of political economy to a legislature; Ricardian political economy was not a branch of the statesman's craft, but a science in its own right, which described the laws of production and distribution in the national economy. This was the second crucial step in our history.

Ricardo's concern with distribution also coloured his analysis of the international economy. His arguments led the political economist to think of trade between states in relation to developmental themes, such as the effects of progress on distribution and population-wage dynamics. This led us to argue that Ricardo's elaboration of comparative advantage as the basis for trade between nations had important implications for how international trade was conceptualized. In short, in view of Ricardo's analysis a system of nation-states was a sub-optimal arrangement for the accumulation of international wealth, because although national borders were non-economic in nature, they still acted as containers of economic phenomena – capital and labour. Ricardo's arguments therefore made it possible to think of the world as subjected to two divergent forces: the economic and the political. Economics continuously allocated resources according to cost differentials, whereas nation states reflected the relatively static influence of culture and history.

We brought our history to a close with Ricardo, after realizing this study's primary purpose: to narrate the emergence of the national economy and the international economy as objects of thought. By this, we meant the ability to 'think' these objects using arguments relating to phenomena such as labour, trade, and capital. Our account is partial in several senses: geographically (it focuses on Britain); temporally (it focuses on the early modern period); and thematically (it focuses on theoretical discourses rather than practices of government). This reflects our modest intention, which was to indicate a critical mode for making the national economy and the international economy historically intelligible: not as ontological objects represented with increasing accuracy in the realm of ideas, but as objects of knowledge emerging from practices of knowing and governing. The introductory chapter set out the nature of this critical history in contrast to Karl Polanyi's work, and it is worth offering a restatement of this theme, this time focused around the research of an equally familiar figure, Robert W. Cox. An historicizing and critical ethos was central to Cox's approach to studying international relations,[1] and given the surface similarities with our approach it is important to assess Cox's work and foreground the distinguishing features and stakes of the critical history attempted here.

The fundamental point to bring to attention is that the invocation of change is central to Cox's programme, in two different but related senses. First, change is treated as a fact of human reality, and this means that the concepts of political economy are constantly being outmoded by the world that they are intended to describe. The implication is that theory that is not historically focused is especially susceptible to mistaking contemporary features of the world for enduring or timeless structures. At this point Cox developed a powerful distinction between problem-solving theory and critical theory. The former takes the dominant institutions and power relations in the world as given and tries to optimize their operation, whereas the latter 'stands apart from the prevailing order' to inquire into its origins and to determine if fundamental change is occurring (Cox 1981: 129). We are told that Kenneth Waltz's positivist neo-realism is a case of problem-solving theory that distances itself from history to generate law-like hypotheses regarding international relations, and the history of international relations then acts as a mere data set to refine these hypotheses. Critical theory, as found in certain historicizing strands of historical materialism such as Cox's, instead emphasizes historical change and investigates the way human nature and social structures interact and evolve. Problem-solving theory is therefore comparatively ill-equipped to explain or detect structural change. A good example of structural change is the emergence of the system of states, yet neo-realism is unable to explain its development because this system is presupposed as an historical constant; by contrast, critical theory is preoccupied with historic shifts of exactly this order (Cox and Sinclair 1996: 52–3).

The second sense in which change is central to Cox's work relates not to his historical ontology but to the motivating ethos for critical theory. The assumption of stasis that characterizes problem-solving theory is treated as an 'ideological bias' by Cox, since any existing order will serve some sectional interests (whether national or class) and disadvantage others. Critical theory transcends this bias because it 'allows for a normative choice in favour of a social and political order different from the prevailing order' (Cox 1981: 130). If it is to service this ethical motivation, critical theory must engage in diagnostic work: does the current historical moment contain the seeds of change? Which social actors could achieve change on the necessary scale? (Cox and Sinclair 1996: 54–5.)

The ethical motivations of Cox's critical theory and its ontological presuppositions are realized in his primary unit of analysis: historical structures, or frameworks for action. Cox recommended decomposing a structure into material capabilities, ideas, and institutions, and he developed further distinctions between hegemonic and non-hegemonic structures, and distinguished 'spheres of activity', such as production, state, and world order. A structure is a means to simplify and represent one aspect of a complex world. The analysis of change within a structure can then be linked to the analysis of related structures and their development through time, and in this way critical theory can follow the complex chains of causation that create shifts in world orders (Cox 1981: 135–8).

It is these premises that Cox mobilized in his description of the rise of the liberal order in his sweeping work, *Production, Power, and World Order*. Cox approached the liberal order with the concepts he developed earlier in the book, which included twelve ideal-typical 'modes of social relations of production' (from subsistence to central planning), and a sketch of their links to three historical processes: simple reproduction, capitalism, and redistributive development. Central planning, for example, was a consequence of redistributive development in the Soviet Union (Cox 1987: 84). We need to mark that this is a highly theoretical species of intellectual labour, for Cox's modes represent the attempt to 'translate the general category of production into concepts that express concrete historical forms of the ways in which production has been organized'. In other words, Cox's modes are theoretical categories deduced from another category – 'the general category of production'. Production, in turn, is derived from a Polanyian philosophical anthropology that elevates work as the universal 'transformation of nature for the purpose of satisfying human needs and desires', so that the 'concept of production relations covers the whole universe of work' (ibid.: 1, 13–14). This descending hierarchy – from the general notion of work through production to modes of social relations of production – is joined to a complementary ascending hierarchy from modes through states to world orders. States are said to influence modes of social relations of production, and different forms of state will correspond to different world orders (ibid.: 105–9). Having erected this conceptual edifice through intense abstractional activity, Cox then turned to the history of the liberal order.

Here Cox's general argument is that a system of states had arrived by the Peace of Westphalia and evolved mercantilism and the balance of power as its operating procedures. This order was replaced when the British bourgeoisie achieved political hegemony internally and the British state achieved military and financial hegemony externally – the 'liberal state and the liberal world order emerged together'. Prior to the liberal order, the 'world economy was constrained within political boundaries laid down by states', but by the middle of the nineteenth century the 'world economy achieved autonomy, such that its own laws began to constrain state policies' (ibid.: 107, 123). A key mechanism for change was the calibration of state actions and bourgeois interests as a whole in Britain, especially in relation to the institutional framework and foreign policy. Bourgeois dominance saw the creation of markets for labour at the same time as labour agitation was suppressed, and free trade trumped formal empire as the goal of external negotiations. As an object of desire for the hegemonic class of the world hegemon, the enterprise labour market became the dominant mode of social relations of production in early capitalism, and a liberal world order provided the external conditions for its expansion. Key among these conditions was a split between politics and economics, in the sense that the state and state system were to guarantee the operation of the 'open world economy' but refrain from interfering in its actual distributive mechanisms (ibid.: 127, 149–50). In this context, Cox treated political economy as the key ideological manifestation of the rise of the bourgeoisie and the coming of the liberal order. For example, Adam Smith is said to have provided the intellectual rationale for the autonomous liberal state that facilitated markets by removing mercantile obstructions and producing public goods, while David Ricardo articulated liberal doctrine on currency (ibid.: 129–34). World orders, states, and modes of social relations of production are thus tied together in Cox's narrative to account for the emergence of the liberal order and its effects.

The primary problem with this narrative is that historical investigation is subordinated to the requirements of an abstract and pre-determined theoretical framework, and as a consequence history acts as mere grist to the theoretical mill – ironically a version of the ahistorical deficiency that Cox claimed to identify in Waltz. To put it more explicitly, before inquiry even begins, it is already determined that structures will be found operating at three different levels – modes, states, and world orders – and that there will be a succession of correlated changes to new instances of these structures that are driven by the structures themselves. The tautological character of this approach follows from its ethical commitment to change and the corresponding attempt to capture transition not in terms of open-ended contextual description but through epochal shifts in theoretically postulated unities, 'historical structures'. In this context we can note three points of divergence between Cox's narrative and our own critical history.

The first is Cox's reliance on mercantilism as a category to describe political economy before Smith. We have shown though that mercantilism was a highly

tendentious and anachronistic construction produced by Smith, and that it continues to obfuscate some two hundred years later is perfect evidence of Smith's
rhetorical triumph. The actual forms of argument and programmes of government
advanced by 'mercantilist' authors – including the complex calculations regarding the security–wealth nexus, their implications for state policy, and their mode
of insertion into practices of government – remain below the level of abstraction
at which Cox's history operates. Second, and continuing this line, Cox viewed
Smith as anticipating the coming liberal order, while we portrayed Smith as an
author contributing to a tradition of manuals for statesmen who achieved limited
influence in his lifetime. In contrast to Smith's work, Ricardian political economy concerned itself with questions of class distribution in isolation from the
presuppositions of the state administration tradition, and this new science was
both mobilized and denounced by politicians. At this point, our history would lead
us to emphasize the complex mix of rationalities informing government, for we
could point to at least three rival species of counsel (analysis of interest, political
œconomy, Ricardian political economy), and the variegated relationships between
counsellors and the work of government (citizen pamphleteers, university aca-
demics, politician-economists). In Cox's account, this complexity was reduced to
the singular expression of dominant class interests in the form of 'liberal' reason
of state. Finally, we can note the diverging accounts of the split between politics and economics, and of the international economy: Cox posited the former as
inherent to the liberal order and the second as a reality achieved in the liberal
epoch once the vestiges of mercantilism were swept away. By contrast, our critical approach led us to instead treat the international economy as an intellectual
object formed in certain species of counsel (political œconomy, political economy)
and presupposed by their programs for government (a system of liberty, reform of
the Corn Laws); within these programmes a split between politics and economics
was *projected*, one that sometimes found anchorage in governmental practice, and
sometimes did not.

Our history was thus concerned to investigate multiple genres of counsel in a
contextual manner and to describe their programmatic attempts to manage trade
and wealth. This approach allowed us to engage with these authors without suc-
cumbing to several temptations: first, accepting their rhetorical constructions at
face value (mercantilism); second, assuming that the rise and fall of genres of
counsel was indicative of epochal shifts in basic structures (the liberal state); and
third, conflating theoretical objects with referents in the world (the autonomous
international economy). This is the sense in which our history claims to be critical.

It should be clear that this is a different sense to that intended by Cox, where
'critical' refers to an ethical motivation in relation to the present and the hope
that seismic political-economic shifts are at hand. As we noted, the Coxian theorist is to diagnose the present in order to facilitate strategic political action. Cox's
label for his approach, 'critical theory', is therefore perfectly apt, and provides a
useful contrast with our label of 'critical history', which is not intended to proph-
esy change but to illuminate the intellectual processes that inform contemporary
practices of governing and knowing. This is one of the points at which Foucault's

work has been most influential, for while he was at times closer to critical theory than critical history,[2] his sentiment that historical research can and should reveal the paths of development and entanglement of contemporary arrangements can nevertheless be fully endorsed (for example, Foucault 1990: 11–3).

Our critical history was not devoid of theoretical assumptions – as we saw in the Introduction, several theoretical moves were necessary to clear a path for our empirical enquiry – but critical history is methodologically agnostic with respect to the need for political change. In fact, historical study could well produce results that lead one to evaluate current institutions as valuable accomplishments. In this regard, we can note that the split between politics and economics that is presumed and projected by a number of contemporary discourses, such as neoclassical economics, has been resented in ideologies both left and right. We should recall, however, that a version of this split provided the basis for representing the human and non-human materials so voraciously consumed by the fiscal-military state as valuable on non-militaristic grounds, as productive labour and capital. From here, authors such as Mill and Ricardo attempted to contest security-centric foreign policy by drawing attention to its economic costs. More explicitly, the politics-economics split fostered a powerful set of arguments that were used to contest the pre-eminence of national security as an object of governmental concern, and we need only look at recent debates in the United States regarding the cost of the wars in Afghanistan and Iraq to see that economic arguments continue to jostle with arguments from national security. We might therefore think that the politics-economics split provides a valuable ideological function in contemporary political life. Critical history is unable to provide an answer one way or the other to questions of this type, but it can clarify the historical contexts and contests relevant to posing the question, which is a pre-condition for giving credible answers within the discipline of political economy and without.

Notes

Introduction

1 See Blyth (2002).
2 For Polanyi's philosophical framework, and its points of instability, see Block (2003).
3 For key readings of Foucault in these terms, see Rajchman (1985: 50–60), and Veyne (1997).
4 See also Walter (2008).
5 See Fitzgibbons (1995); Hont (2005); Hont and Ignatieff (1983); Montes (2004); Pocock (1985, 2003); Teichgraeber (1986); and Winch (1978).
6 Note Pocock's analogous remark that the late eighteenth-century shift in relation to commerce lies outside the model of "virtues, rights, and manners" (Pocock 1985: 37). See also his discussion of how the institutions of Leviathan (standing army and public credit) came to be imbued with "greater significance than Leviathan himself" (Pocock 1996: 98).
7 This has issued in multiple divergent attempts, for example, mainstream political economy (Gilpin 2001); empire (Hardt and Negri 2000); globalization (Ōmae 1995); and world-systems theory (Wallerstein 1974).

1 Counsellors to government

1 The story is complicated by the fact that, while notions of counselling were carried by Italian civic humanism, the obstacles of the English intellectual context also needed to be navigated, including the operation of the Ancient Constitution as a powerful ideology. See Pocock (2003: 333–60).
2 See also Lehmberg (1961).
3 See Slaughter (1984: xi); and Condren (1993).
4 Steuart did not use the ligature "œ" as Smith did, and contemporary reprints often modernize the spelling. The spelling of the referenced text is followed throughout this book. For the significance, see Tribe (1978: Chapter 5). For patriarchalism in early modern political thought more generally, see Schochet (1975).
5 This is one of Foucault's favourite hypotheses, and we will suggest some revisions to it in Chapter 3.

2 Genres of counsel and the administrative state

1 Note that Skinner has recently moved away from this epochal rendering in favour of underlining continued contest over the concept of the state. See Skinner (2009).
2 See Bireley (1995).
3 See generally Pincus (1996) and Scott (2000) for the seventeenth century and Thompson (2006) for the eighteenth.
4 See Hicks (1987). Note that the second and greater part of Rohan's *Treatise* consisted of historical examples.

5 The trade with France was a sensitive issue because it was perceived to be a losing trade for England. See Priestley (1951).

6 See Endres (1985). Note also Cookson's reminder, that we must not assume that the technical crudity of political arithmetic's estimates "deprived them of influence on contemporary opinion" (Cookson 1983: 48).

7 We can suspect that Hume meant police to refer to a type of governmental activity that was more expansive than crime detecting by an armed constabulary. William Blackstone's sense may be more appropriate, for whom "public police and oeconomy" meant "the due regulation and domestic order of the kingdom", in which "individuals of the state" were "like members of a well governed family" (Blackstone 1778: Vol. IV: 162). On this view, Hume's police would share considerable territory with Mun's "policy". Notice also how the patriarchal household provided an accommodating metaphor for imagining the work of state administration, since we saw how important it was for James Steuart's political œconomy in Chapter 1.

8 As we would expect, since Mun's pamphlet was probably written in 1630 (Schumpeter 1954a: 356), pre-dating the arrival of Rohan's analysis in England.

9 See Foucault's lectures 11 and 12 on this theme (Foucault 2007: 255–332).

3 The state's strength and wealth

1 For the fiscal-military state see also Chapters 5 and 6 of Braddick (2000).

2 Note Eli Hecksher's comment on this point, that it was "interesting as a proof of how important considerations of power in money policy appeared even to so advanced a rationalist as Locke" (Heckscher 1935: Vol. I: 47).

3 This might be thought of as a representation of the discursive mechanics that underlay the "general acceptance of the existence of harmony and mutual support between the pursuit of power and the pursuit of plenty" (Viner 1948: 10–11).

4 As Coleman noted, the balance of trade functioned as a maxim or rule of thumb (Coleman 1980: 786).

5 The common law tradition has been central to this understanding of the English nation. Consider the following claim from John Davies, that the common law was "so framed and fitted to the nature and disposition of this people, as we may properly say it is connatural to the Nation, so as it cannot possibly be ruled by any other Law" (quoted in Pocock 1987: 33). For a survey of sumptuary law see Hunt (1996).

6 While it is certainly fair to claim that luxury was a matter of great concern in republican disquisitions on virtue (Pocock 2003: Chapter 13), we should remember that it was primarily in relation to circulation that luxury was apprehended by counsel on trade.

7 In France, the physiocrats pushed the land-as-origin view to its limit, insisting that manufactures were "barren" as a contribution to circulation. See (Mirabeau 1766).

8 See Tribe (1978: 91–3) for a similar discussion of Richard Cantillon.

9 This is dubious, for it is rather the case that the Thirty Years War spurred elaborations of sovereignty models as a means for ending confessional conflict, see Hunter (2001). Schumpeter offered an assessment similar to Foucault's in relation to German economic literature (Schumpeter 1954b: 31).

10 See Burchell (1991) and Gordon (1991: 14–27).

4 Strength, wealth, and state rivalry

1 See Koenigsberger (1989) and Robertson (1994).

2 For the constitutional issues, see Greene (1990) and Pocock (1995).

3 See Chapters 3 and 4 of Knorr (1944) for a valuable survey of titles that are construed as having embodied the imperial orthodoxy before American independence.

4 And institutional contest over the sources of colonial government. For a survey of these issues, see Steele (1998).

5 See Hutchison (1988, 126–9) and Viner (1937: 79–83).

6 On this theme, see Hont's magisterial *Jealousy of Trade*, especially the long Introduction (Hont 2005).
7 For the providence theme in international trade theory, including its coupling with free trade, see Chapter 2 of Viner (1976).

5 Smith and the economy

1 This suggests Smith took this material from the French *Encyclopédie*. See Rashid (1990: 4).
2 See, for example, Marx (1951: 148–75) and Schumpeter (1954a: 192, n22).
3 In this context, note Cookson's comment that Smith's arguments provided "a conceptual framework to which anxieties about the increasing cost of war were easily attached" (Cookson 1983: 38).
4 On abstraction as an object of historical inquiry, see Chapter 1 of Pocock (2009).
5 This reading draws on (Tribe 2006).
6 See the powerful discussion in (Tribe 1978: 102–4).
7 See Tribe (2006: 64).
8 For sympathy in Smith, see Fitzgibbons (1995: 62–6); Haakonssen (1981: Chapter 3); and Phillipson (1983). Elements of the intellectual context are described in Force (2003: Chapter 1) and Raphael (2007: Chapter 4).
9 Smith also refused the view of those who held "republican principles" and had been "jealous of a standing army as dangerous to liberty". On the contrary, Smith suggested that when a military force was under the command of those who had an interest in supporting civil authority, a standing army could even "be favourable to liberty" (Smith 1981 [1776]: Vol. II: 706–7).
10 We can therefore endorse Schumpeter's claim that the consultant administrators were one of Smith's sources (Schumpeter 1954a: 184). See also Tribe (1978, 107–9). For the statesman in Smith, see Haakonssen (1981: Chapter 4); Winch (1996: 90–123). Peter McNamara's comparison of Smith and Alexander Hamilton on statesmanship is also revealing (McNamara 1998).
11 See Holmes (1990).
12 See, for example, Becker (1996).

6 Smith and the international economy

1 As Blecker pointed out in the context of his intelligent reconstruction of Smith's arguments in the light of contemporary economic theory, in *Wealth of Nations* "the concepts of value, productivity and profitability are all conflated" (Blecker 1997: 531). As noted, judgements of this type are outside our brief.
2 For a critical look at mercantilism as a category and Smith's role in its genesis, see Coleman (1980).
3 Here Smith invoked the metaphor of the household that we discussed in Chapter 1.
4 As Viner claimed, it was significant that Smith forced the issue by presenting a choice between defence and opulence. See Viner (1948: 17).
5 This point becomes more significant when read alongside Hont's suggestion that the division of labour represented Smith's solution to the rich country–poor country debate. See Hont (2005: 302–3).
6 Smith was referring here to "the contest with America". Fortunately for Britain, the "disorder" and the resulting loss of trade were mitigated by five unforseen and compensating events (Smith 1981 [1776]: Vol. II: 606–7).
7 Winch (1996: Chapter 4) described Smith's commitment to "the wisdom of Solon"; in short, the legislator was "like Solon, when he cannot establish the best system of laws, he will endeavour to establish the best that the people can bear" (Smith 1982 [1759]: 233). In relation to Smith's proposal for union, however, we might wonder if this quality was not lacking.

8 See Hont (2005: 305).
9 Although Gervaise and Smith had some elements in common, especially the autonomy they gave to the analysis of trade between states, we can appreciate their differences by remembering that Gervaise treated states as "but certain quantities of men" with certain geographical characteristics, which then attracted an appropriate quantity of money. The administrative character of Smith therefore had no counterpart in Gervaise, just as Smith did not share Gervaise's fiscal-military concern with the quantity of money and men.
10 Here the structuring role of natural jurisprudence in Smith's thought seems to be central. See Haakonssen (1981) and Teichgraeber (1986). Thomas Pownall emphasized experience over system in his long letter to Smith – one of the few serious engagements with Smith's work following its original publication – in which he at times reprimanded Smith on exactly this basis (Pownall 1987 [1776]).
11 Foucault famously jibed that Marxism did not represent a discontinuity because it was only a variation on a Ricardian theme, namely, a teleological rendering of the interplay of time and anthropology. See Foucault (2002: 284–5).

7 Ricardo and the national economy

1 See Rashid (1982); Teichgraeber (1987); and Tribe (1995b).
2 Mill also followed Smith in making the division of labour crucial to the accumulation of wealth, and registered a caveat against agriculture in favour of manufacturing (Mill 1965 [1808]: 29). Thus, the same tension that appeared in Smith – between the position of agriculture as the most rewarding species of labour, but least susceptible to improvement by the division of labour – also appeared in Mill. This tension was ultimately resolved in favour of agriculture through the analysis of the employments of capital, just as it was in *Wealth of Nations*.
3 Torrens also used a version of the division of labour doctrine to conceive of wealth accumulation: because the land and water were not subject to increase, only labour could be increased, and this occurred through the division of labour. The first type of division was termed mechanical, and it referred to the division of labour between discrete tasks; the second was called territorial, and it referred to the division of labour between locations (Torrens 1993 [1808]: 7–9).
4 See Tribe's (1978) Chapter 6 for a discussion of pamphlets from the same year by Malthus, Torrens, and West, which similarly broke with the preceding forms of argument, albeit less radically than Ricardo.
5 As Sraffa argued (2004b, xxxi–xxxii), the architectural reason for this claim, which Ricardo never made explicit, was that the *Essay* was a corn model. That is, in agriculture, corn was treated as both a capital input (as wages) and an output, whereas other trades were obliged to use agricultural output as an input. Agriculture was therefore treated as a unique sector where profits were simply a ratio between input and output, and this allowed the problem of value to be elided. This elegance was lost by the shift away from a corn model in the *Principles*, hence its troubled Chapter 1: "On Value", where labour was made to explain the formation of value. Note that this interpretation is a point of controversy. See Hollander (1973) and Peach (1993: 39–86).
6 See Sraffa (2004b: xxx–xxxvii).
7 Although at other places, Smith treated rent as a cost of production. See Winch (1996: 351).

8 Ricardo and the international economy

1 But note Pocock (1987: 247–8).
2 Ricardo's claim to precedence has been an ongoing topic of contest. See, for example, Ruffin (2002); Seligman and Hollander (1911); and Viner (1937: 441–4).
3 For the implications that a straightforward reading of Ricardo's numerical example has for international trade theory, see Maneschi (2004).

4 This shift is, perhaps, parallel to political economy's migration from the generalist's domain of publicly available pamphlets and books to the specialist's university degree. See Tribe (2005).
5 Schumpeter made a similar diagnosis, describing the "Ricardian vice" as the tendency to use abstract reasoning as the basis for policy (Schumpeter 1954a: 473).

9 Conclusion

1 And both elements have been central to more recent calls for a revitalized political economy, see Amin and Palan (1996); Amoore *et al.* (2000).
2 See Hindess (1997: 269–70); Hunter (1991: 42–7).

Bibliography

Primary sources

Anonymous (1657) *An Exact Abridgment of Publick Acts and Ordinances of Parliament, Made from the Year 1640 to the Year 1656*, London.

— (1664) *The Dutch Drawn to the Life*, London.

— (1697) *Some Short Considerations Concerning the State of the Nation*.

— (1720) *The Interest of the Nation Asserted. Being a Defence of the Woollen and Silk Manufactures, Against Some Notions in a Late Pamphlet, Said to be Writ by the Famous Mr. Laws*, London.

— (1759) *An Account of the Constitution and Present State of Great Britain, Together with a View of its Trade, Policy, and Interest, Respecting Other Nations, & of the Principal Curiosities of Great Britain and Ireland*, London.

— (1794) *An Essay on the Happiness and Advantages of a Well-Ordered Family, Respecting the Present and Future Welfare of its Members*, London.

Arbuthnot, John (1745) *An Essay on the Usefulness of Mathematical Learning. In a Letter From a Gentleman in the City, to his Friend at Oxford*, 3rd edn, London.

Bacon, Francis (1661) *A Letter of Advice Written by Sir. Francis Bacon to the Duke of Buckingham, When he Became Favourite to King James*, London.

Barbon, Nicholas (1690) *A Discourse of Trade*, London.

— (1696) *A Discourse Concerning Coining the New Money Lighter*, London.

Bell, William (1756) *A Dissertation on the Following Subject: What Causes Principally Contribute to Render a Nation Populous? And What Effect has the Populousness of a Nation on its Trade?* Cambridge.

Bentham, Jeremy (1952 [1793–95]) *Manual of Political Economy*, in W. Stark (ed.) *Jeremy Bentham's Economic Writings*, 3 vols, London: Allen & Unwin, vol. 1, pp. 219-74.

— (1954 [1801–4]) *Institute of Political Economy*, in W. Stark (ed.) *Jeremy Bentham's Economic Writings*, 3 vols, London: Allen & Unwin, vol. 3, pp. 303–80.

Bethel, Slingsby (1671) *The Present Interest of England Stated. By a Lover of his King and Countrey*, London.

— (1673) *Observations on the Letter Written to Sir Thomas Osborn, Upon the Reading of a Book Called 'The Present Interest of England Stated'*, London.

— (1677) *The Present State of Christendome and the Interest of England, With a Regard to France*, London.

Blackstone, William (1778) *Commentaries on the Laws of England*, 4 vols, 8th edn, Oxford.

Bolingbroke, Henry St John (1970 [1752]) *Letters on the Study and Use of History*, 2 vols, New York: Garland.

Botero, Giovanni (1956 [1589]) *The Reason of State*, trans. P. J. Waley and D. P. Waley, London: Routledge and Kegan Paul.

Campbell, John (1734) *A View of the Dangers to Which the Trade of Great-Britain to Turkey and Italy will be Exposed, if Naples and Sicily Fall into the Hands of the Spaniards*, London.

Cantillon, Philip (1759) *The Analysis of Trade, Commerce, Coin, Bullion, Banks, and Foreign Exchanges*, London.

Capper, Benjamin Pitts (1801) *A Statistical Account of the Population and Cultivation, Produce and Consumption, of England and Wales*, London.

Cavendish, William (1984 [1659]) 'Newcastle's advice to Charles II', in Thomas P. Slaughter (ed.) *Ideology and Politics on the Eve of Restoration: Newcastle's Advice to Charles II*, Philadelphia, PA: American Philosophical Society.

Child, Josiah (1668) *Brief Observations Concerning Trade, and Interest of Money*, London.

— (1690) *A Discourse About Trade Wherein the Reduction of Interest in Money to 4 l. Per Centum, is Recommended*, London.

Clement, Simon (1695) *A Discourse of the General Notions of Money, Trade, & Exchanges*, London.

Davenant, Charles (1696) *An Essay on the East-India-Trade*, London.

— (1698) *Discourses on the Publick Revenues, and on the Trade of England*, 2 vols, London.

— (1715) *An Account of the Trade Between Great-Britain, France, Holland, Spain, Portugal, Italy, Africa, Newfoundland, &c.*, London.

— (1942 [1695]) 'A memorial concerning the coyn of England', in Abbott Payson Usher (ed.) *Two Manuscripts*, Baltimore, MD: Johns Hopkins University Press.

de Britaine, William (1672) *The Interest of England in the Present War with Holland*, London.

Defoe, Daniel (1728a) *A Plan of the English Commerce*, London.

— (1728b) *Some Considerations on the Reasonableness and Necessity of Encreasing and Encouraging the Seamen*, London.

— (1729) *The Advantages of Peace and Commerce*, London.

— (1965 [1705]) *Defoe's Review*, 22 vols, ed. Arthur Wellesley Secord, New York: AMS Press.

Du Moulin, Peter (1673) *Englands Appeal from the Private Cabal at White-Hall to the Great Council of the Nation, the Lords and Commons in Parliament Assembled*.

Fortrey, Samuel (1713) *Englands Interest Consider'd, in the Increase of the Trade of this Kingdom*, London.

Gee, Joshua (1729) *The Trade and Navigation of Great-Britain Considered*, London.

Gervaise, Isaac (1720) *The System or Theory of the Trade of the World*, London.

Graunt, John (1973 [1662]) 'Natural and political observations made upon the bills of mortality', in Peter Laslett (ed.) *The Earliest Classics: John Graunt and Gregory King*, Farnborough, Hants: Gregg.

Harris, Joseph (1757) *An Essay upon Money and Coins*, London.

Harvey, William (1963 [1636]) *The Circulation of the Blood, and Other Writings*, London.

Hill, Joseph (1673) *The Interest of these United Provinces*, Middleburg.

Hobbes, Thomas (1991 [1651]) *Leviathan*, ed. Richard Tuck, Cambridge: Cambridge University Press.

Hume, David (1985 [1777]) *Essays, Moral, Political, and Literary*, ed. Eugene F. Miller, Indianapolis: Liberty Classics.

King, Gregory (1973 [1696]) 'Natural and political observations and conclusions upon the state and condition of England 1696', in Peter Laslett (ed.) *The Earliest Classics: John Graunt and Gregory King*, Farnborough, Hants: Gregg.

Law, John (1720) *Money and Trade Consider'd; With a Proposal for Supplying the Nation with Money*, 2nd edn, London.

Locke, John (1991) *Locke on Money*, 2 vols, ed. Patrick Hyde Kelly, Oxford: Clarendon Press.

Macburney, James (1701) *A Letter to an Honourable Member of the House of Commons. Briefly Shewing, the Wealth, Power and Strength, that the Hollanders and other Nations Gain, by Fishing on the Coasts and Seas of Great Britain*, London.

Massie, J. (1760) *A Representation Concerning the Knowledge of Commerce as a National Concern*, London.

McWard, Robert (1672) *The English Ballance, Weighing the Reasons, of Englands Present Conjunction with France, Against the Dutch*.

Mildmay, William (1765) *The Laws and Policy of England*, London.

Mill, James (1965 [1808]) *Commerce Defended*, New York: Augustus M. Kelley.

Mirabeau, Victor de Riquetti Marquis de (1766) *The Oeconomical Table, an Attempt Towards Ascertaining and Exhibiting the Source, Progress, and Employment of Riches*, London.

Mortimer, Thomas (1772) *The Elements of Commerce, Politics and Finances*, London.

Mun, Thomas (1928 [1664]) *England's Treasure by Forraign Trade*, Oxford: Blackwell.

Newton, Benjamin (1756) *Another Dissertation on the Mutual Support of Trade and Civil Liberty*, London.

North, Dudley (1669) *Observations and Advices Oeconomical*, London.

Paterson, William (1694) *A Brief Account of the Intended Bank of England*, London.

— (1858 [1701]) *The Writings of William Paterson*, 2 vols, ed. Saxe Bannister, London: Effingham Wilson.

Petty, William (1690) *Political Arithmetick*, London.

— (1691) *The Political Anatomy of Ireland. With the Establishment for that Kingdom when the Late Duke of Ormond was Lord Lieutenant. Taken from the Records. To which is Added Verbum Sapienti; or An Account of the Wealth and Expences of England, and the Method of Raising Taxes in the Most Equal Manner*, London.

Pollexfen, John (1697) *England and East-India Inconsistent in their Manufactures*, London.

Pownall, Thomas (1765) *The Administration of the Colonies*, 2nd edn, London.

— (1987 [1776]) 'A letter from Governor Pownall to Adam Smith', in Ernest Campbell Mossner and Ian Simpson Ross (eds) *The Glasgow Edition of the Works and Correspondence of Adam Smith: The Correspondence of Adam Smith*, Indianapolis: Liberty Fund.

Ricardo, David (2004 [1815]) *An Essay on the Influence of a Low Price of Corn on the Profits of Stock*, in Piero Sraffa (ed.) *The Works and Correspondence of David Ricardo*, 11 vols, Indianapolis: Liberty Fund, vol. 4, pp. 1–41.

— (2004 [1817]) *On the Principles of Political Economy and Taxation*, in Piero Sraffa (ed.) *The Works and Correspondence of David Ricardo*, Indianapolis: Liberty Fund, vol. 1.

— (2004 [1819–21]) *Letters: 1819 – June 1821*, in Piero Sraffa (ed.) *The Works and Correspondence of David Ricardo*, Indianapolis: Liberty Fund, vol. 8.

Rohan, Henri duc de (1641) *A Treatise of the Interest of the Princes and States of Christendome Written in French by the Duke of Rohan; Englished by H.H*, London.

Rolt, Richard (1756) *A New Dictionary of Trade and Commerce*, London.

Senior, Nassau William (1951 [1836]) *An Outline of the Science of Political Economy*, 7th edn, New York: A. M. Kelley.

Smith, Adam (1981 [1776]) *An Inquiry into the Nature and Causes of the Wealth of Nations*, 2 vols. Andrew S. Skinner, R.H. Campbell and W.B. Todd (eds), Indianapolis: Liberty Classics.

— (1982 [1759]) *The Theory of Moral Sentiments*. D.D. Raphael and A.L. Macfie (eds), Indianapolis: Liberty Fund.

Smith, Thomas (1969 [1581]) *A Discourse of the Commonweal of this Realm of England*, ed. Mary Dewar, Charlottesville, VA: University Press of Virginia.

Steuart, James (1767) *An Inquiry into the Principles of Political Oeconomy*, 2 vols, London.

Stewart, Dugald (1854–60) *The Collected Works of Dugald Stewart*, 11 vols, ed. Sir William Hamilton, Edinburgh: T. Constable and Co.

Temple, William (1758) *A Vindication of Commerce and the Arts; Proving that they are the Source of the Greatness, Power, Riches and Populousness of a State*, London.

Torrens, Robert (1993 [1808]) *The Economists Refuted and Other Early Economic Writings*, ed. Peter Groenewegen, Fairfield, NJ: Augustus M. Kelley.

Tucker, Josiah (1755) *The Elements of Commerce, and Theory of Taxes*, Bristol.

Vanderlint, Jacob (1734) *Money Answers All Things*, London.

Webster, William (1740) *The Consequences of Trade, as to the Wealth and Strength of any Nation*, London.

Wood, William (1718) *A Survey of Trade*, London.

Young, Arthur (1771) *Proposals to the Legislature for Numbering the People*, London.

Secondary sources

Abdelal, Rawi (2007) *Capital Rules: The Construction of Global Finance*, Cambridge, MA: Harvard University Press.

Amin, Ash and Palan, Ronen (1996) 'Theme: historicizing international political economy', *Review of International Political Economy* 3(2): 209–15.

Amoore, Louise, Dodgson, Richard, Germain, Randall D., Gills, Barry K., Langley, Paul, and Watson, Iain (2000) 'Paths to a historicized international political economy', *Review of International Political Economy* 7(1): 53–71.

Armitage, David (1995) 'The Scottish vision of empire: intellectual origins of the Darien Venture', in John Robertson (ed.) *A Union for Empire: Political Thought and the British Union of 1707*, Cambridge: Cambridge University Press, pp. 97–118.

— (2000) *The Ideological Origins of the British Empire*, Cambridge: Cambridge University Press.

Ashley, Maurice (1934) *Financial and Commercial Policy under the Cromwellian Protectorate*, London: Oxford University Press.

Aubrey, John (1975) *Brief Lives*, ed. Richard Barber, London: Folio Society.

Baugh, Daniel A. (1965) *British Naval Administration in the Age of Walpole*, Princeton, NJ: Princeton University Press.

Becker, Gary (1996) *Accounting for Tastes*, Cambridge, MA: Harvard University Press.

Bireley, Robert (1995) 'Scholasticism and reason of state', in Artemio Enzo (ed.) *Aristotelismo politico e ragion di Stato: atti del convegno internazionale di Torino, 11–13 febbraio 1993*, Firenze: L.S. Olschki.

Blecker, Robert A. (1997) 'The "unnatural and retrograde order": Adam Smith's theories of trade and development reconsidered', *Economica* 64(255): 527–37.

Block, Fred (2003) 'Karl Polanyi and the writing of *The Great Transformation*', *Theory and Society* 32(3): 275–306.

Blyth, Mark (2002) *Great Transformations: Economic Ideas and Institutional Change in the Twentieth Century*, New York: Cambridge University Press.

Braddick, M. J. (2000) *State Formation in Early Modern England, c. 1550–1700*, Cambridge: Cambridge University Press.

Brewer, John (1990) *The Sinews of Power: War, Money, and the English State, 1688–1783*, Cambridge, MA: Harvard University Press.

— (1994) 'The eighteenth-century British state: contexts and issues', in Lawrence Stone (ed.) *An Imperial State at War: Britain from 1689 to 1815*, London: Routledge, pp. 52–71.

Buck, Peter (1982) 'People who counted: political arithmetic in the eighteenth century', *Isis* 73(1): 28–45.

Burchell, Graham (1991) 'Peculiar interests: civil society and governing "the system of natural liberty"', in Graham Burchell, Colin Gordon and Peter Miller (eds)

The Foucault Effect: Studies in Governmentality, London: Harvester Wheatsheaf, pp. 119–50.

Çalışkan, Koray and Callon, Michel (2009) 'Economization, Part 1: shifting attention from the economy towards processes of economization', *Economy and Society* 38(3): 369–98.

Callon, Michel (1998) 'An essay on framing and overflowing: economic externalities revisited by sociology', in Michel Callon (ed.) *The Laws of the Markets*, Oxford: Blackwell, pp. 244–69.

Caspari, Fritz (1954) *Humanism and the Social Order in Tudor England*, Chicago: University of Chicago Press.

Coleman, D. C. (1980) 'Mercantilism revisited', *The Historical Journal* 23(4): 773–91.

Condren, Conal (1993) 'Casuistry to Newcastle: "The Prince" in the world of the book', in Nicholas Phillipson and Quentin Skinner (eds) *Political Discourse in Early Modern Britain*, Cambridge: Cambridge University Press, pp. 164–86.

— (2006) *Argument and Authority in Early Modern England: The Presupposition of Oaths and Offices*, Cambridge: Cambridge University Press.

Cookson, J. E. (1983) 'Political arithmetic and war in Britain, 1793–1815', *War and Society* 1(2): 37–60.

Cox, Robert W. (1981) 'Social forces, states and world orders: beyond international relations theory', *Millennium* 10(2): 126–55.

— (1987) *Production, Power, and World Order: Social Forces in the Making of History*, New York: Columbia University Press.

Cox, Robert W. with Sinclair, Timothy J. (1996) *Approaches to World Order*, Cambridge: Cambridge University Press.

de Goede, Marieke (2005) *Virtue, Fortune and Faith: A Genealogy of Finance*, Minneapolis, Minn: University of Minnesota Press.

Dull, Jonathan R. (1975) *The French Navy and American Independence: A Study of Arms and Diplomacy, 1774–1787*, Princeton, NJ: Princeton University Press.

Elliott, J. H. (1992) 'A Europe of composite monarchies', *Past and Present* 137: 48–71.

Elton, G. R. (1953) *The Tudor Revolution in Government: Administrative Changes in the Reign of Henry VIII*, Cambridge: Cambridge University Press.

Endres, A. M. (1985) 'The functions of numerical data in the writings of Graunt, Petty, and Davenant', *History of Political Economy* 17(2): 245–64.

Ferguson, Arthur B. (1965) *The Articulate Citizen and the English Renaissance*, Durham, NC: Duke University Press.

Finkelstein, Andrea (2000) *Harmony and the Balance: An Intellectual History of Seventeenth-Century English Economic Thought*, Ann Arbor, MI: University of Michigan Press.

Fitzgibbons, Athol (1995) *Adam Smith's System of Liberty, Wealth, and Virtue: The Moral and Political Foundations of the Wealth of Nations*, Oxford: Clarendon Press.

Fontana, Biancamaria (1985) *Rethinking the Politics of Commercial Society: The Edinburgh Review, 1802–1832*, Cambridge: Cambridge University Press.

Force, Pierre (2003) *Self-interest before Adam Smith: A Genealogy of Economic Science*, Cambridge: Cambridge University Press.

Foucault, Michel (1990) *The History of Sexuality*. Vol. 1: *The Will to Knowledge*, trans. Robert Hurley. London: Penguin Books.

— (2002) *The Order of Things: An Archaeology of the Human Sciences*, London: Routledge.

— (2006) *History of Madness*, ed. Jean Khalfa, trans. Jonathan Murphy and Jean Khalfa, London: Routledge.

— (2007) *Security, Territory, Population: Lectures at the Collège de France, 1977–78*, ed. Michel Senellart, trans. Graham Burchell, Basingstoke: Palgrave Macmillan.

— (2008) *The Birth of Biopolitics: Lectures at the Collège de France, 1978–79*, ed. Michel Senellart, trans. Graham Burchell, Basingstoke: Palgrave Macmillan.

Gilpin, Robert (1987) *The Political Economy of International Relations*, Princeton, NJ: Princeton University Press.
— (2001) *Global Political Economy: Understanding the International Economic Order*, Princeton, NJ: Princeton University Press.
Gordon, Colin (1991) 'Introduction', in Graham Burchell, Colin Gordon and Peter Miller (eds) *The Foucault Effect: Studies in Governmentality*, London: Harvester Wheatsheaf, pp. 1–51.
Greene, Jack P. (1990) *Peripheries and Center: Constitutional Development in the Extended Polities of the British Empire and the United States, 1607–1788*, New York: W. W. Norton.
Groenewegen, Peter D. (2002) *Eighteenth-Century Economics: Turgot, Beccaria and Smith and Their Contemporaries*, London: Routledge.
Gunn, J. A. W. (1968) '"Interest will not lie": a seventeenth-century political maxim', *Journal of the History of Ideas* 29(4): 551–64.
— (1969) *Politics and the Public Interest in the Seventeenth Century*, London: Routledge and Kegan Paul.
Guy, John (1995) 'The rhetoric of counsel in early modern England', in Dale Hoak (ed.) *Tudor Political Culture*, Cambridge: Cambridge University Press, pp. 291–310.
Haakonssen, Knud (1981) *The Science of a Legislator: The Natural Jurisprudence of David Hume and Adam Smith*, Cambridge: Cambridge University Press.
Hall, Rodney Bruce (2008) *Central Banking as Global Governance: Constructing Financial Credibility*, Cambridge: Cambridge University Press.
Hardt, Michael and Negri, Antonio (2000) *Empire*, Cambridge, MA: Harvard University Press.
Heckscher, Eli (1935) *Mercantilism*, 2 vols, trans. Mendel Shapiro, London: Allen and Unwin.
Hicks, Philip (1987) 'Bolingbroke, Clarendon, and the role of classical historian', *Eighteenth-Century Studies* 20(4): 445–71.
Hindess, Barry (1997) 'Politics and governmentality', *Economy and Society* 26(2): 257–72.
Hollander, Samuel (1973) 'Ricardo's analysis of the profit rate, 1813–15', *Economica* 40(159): 260–82.
Holmes, Stephen (1990) 'The secret history of self-interest', in Jane J. Mansbridge (ed.) *Beyond Self-Interest*, Chicago: University of Chicago Press, pp. 267–86.
Hont, Istvan (2005) *Jealousy of Trade: International Competition and the Nation State in Historical Perspective*, Cambridge, MA: Harvard University Press.
Hont, Istvan and Ignatieff, Michael (eds) (1983) *Wealth and Virtue: The Shaping of Political Economy in the Scottish Enlightenment*, Cambridge: Cambridge University Press.
Hoppit, Julian (2006) 'The contexts and contours of British economic literature, 1660–1760', *The Historical Journal* 49(1): 79–110.
Houston, Alan Craig (1991) *Algernon Sidney and the Republican Heritage in England and America*, Princeton, N.J.: Princeton University Press.
Hunt, Alan (1996) *Governance of the Consuming Passions: A History of Sumptuary Law*, London: Macmillan.
Hunter, Ian (1991) 'From discourse to dispositif: Foucault and the study of literature', *Meridian* 10(2): 36–53.
— (2001) *Rival Enlightenments: Civil and Metaphysical Philosophy in Early Modern Germany*, Cambridge: Cambridge University Press.
Huntley, Frank Livingstone (1951) 'Sir Thomas Browne, M. D., William Harvey, and the metaphor of the circle', *Bulletin of the History of Medicine* 25: 236–47.
Hutchison, T. W. (1964) *'Positive' Economics and Policy Objectives*, Cambridge, MA: Harvard University Press.
— (1988) *Before Adam Smith: The Emergence of Political Economy, 1662–1776*. Oxford: Basil Blackwell.

Jones, J. R. (1980) *Britain and the World, 1649–1815*, Brighton: Harvester Press.
— (1996) *The Anglo-Dutch Wars of the Seventeenth Century*, London: Longman.
Kennedy, Paul M. (1988) *The Rise and Fall of the Great Powers: Economic Change and Military Conflict from 1500 to 2000*, London: Unwin Hyman.
Knorr, Klaus (1944) *British Colonial Theories, 1570–1850*, Toronto: University of Toronto Press.
Koenigsberger, H. G. (1989) 'Composite states, representative institutions and the American revolution', *Historical Research* 62(148): 135–53.
Lehmberg, Stanford E. (1961) 'English humanists, the reformation and the problem of counsel', *Archiv für Reformationsgeschichte* 52: 74–90.
Letwin, William (1963) *The Origins of Scientific Economics: English Economic Thought, 1660–1776*, London: Methuen.
Lowry, S. Todd (1974) 'The archaeology of the circulation concept in economic theory', *Journal of the History of Ideas* 35(3): 429–44.
MacKenzie, Donald A. (2006) *An Engine, Not a Camera: How Financial Models Shape Markets*, Cambridge, MA: MIT Press.
Mackesy, Piers (1964) *The War for America, 1775–1783*, London: Longman.
Malcolm, Noel (2007) *Reason of State, Propaganda, and the Thirty Years' War: An Unknown Translation by Thomas Hobbes*, Oxford: Clarendon Press.
Maneschi, Andrea (2004) 'The true meaning of David Ricardo's four magic numbers', *Journal of International Economics* 62(2): 433–43.
Marx, Karl (1951) *Theories of Surplus Value*, ed. Karl Kautsky, trans. G. A. Bonner and Emile Burns, London: Lawrence & Wishart.
McNamara, Peter (1998) *Political Economy and Statesmanship: Smith, Hamilton, and the Foundation of the Commercial Republic*, DeKalb, IL: Northern Illinois University Press.
Mears, Natalie (2001) 'Counsel, public debate, and queenship: John Stubbs's "The Discoverie of a Gaping Gulf", 1579', *The Historical Journal* 44(3): 629–50.
Montes, Leonidas (2004) *Adam Smith in Context: A Critical Reassessment of Some Central Components of his Thought*, New York: Palgrave Macmillan.
Neal, Larry (1977) 'Interpreting power and profit in economic history: a case study of the Seven Years' War', *The Journal of Economic History* 37(1): 20–35.
Ōmae, Kenichi (1995) *The End of the Nation State: The Rise of Regional Economies*, New York: Free Press.
Peach, Terry (1993) *Interpreting Ricardo*, Cambridge: Cambridge University Press.
Phillipson, Nicholas (1983) 'Adam Smith as civic moralist', in Istvan Hont and Michael Ignatieff (eds) *Wealth and Virtue: The Shaping of Political Economy in the Scottish Enlightenment*, Cambridge: Cambridge University Press, pp. 179–202.
Pincus, Steven C. A. (1996) *Protestantism and Patriotism: Ideologies and the Making of English Foreign Policy, 1650–1668*, Cambridge: Cambridge University Press.
Pocock, J. G. A. (1985) *Virtue, Commerce, and History: Essays on Political Thought and History, Chiefly in the Eighteenth Century*, Cambridge: Cambridge University Press.
— (1987) *The Ancient Constitution and the Feudal Law: A Study of English Historical Thought in the Seventeenth Century: A Reissue with a Retrospect*, Cambridge: Cambridge University Press.
— (1995) 'Empire, state and confederation: the war of American independence as a crisis in multiple monarchy', in John Robertson (ed.) *A Union for Empire: Political Thought and the British Union of 1707*, Cambridge: Cambridge University Press, pp. 318–48.
— (1996) 'Standing army and public credit: the institutions of Leviathan', in Dale Hoak and Mordechai Feingold (eds) *The World of William and Mary: Anglo-Dutch Perspectives on the Revolution of 1688–89*, Stanford, CA: Stanford University Press, pp. 87–103.
— (2003) *The Machiavellian Moment: Florentine Political Thought and the Atlantic Republican Tradition*, 2nd edn, Princeton, NJ: Princeton University Press.

— (2009) *Political Thought and History: Essays on Theory and Method*, Cambridge: Cambridge University Press.

Polanyi, Karl (1957a) 'The economy as instituted process', in Karl Polanyi, Conrad M. Arensberg and Harry W. Pearson (eds) *Trade and Market in the Early Empires: Economies in History and Theory*, New York: Free Press, pp. 243–70.

— (1957b) 'Aristotle discovers the economy', in Karl Polanyi, Conrad M. Arensberg and Harry W. Pearson (eds) *Trade and Market in the Early Empires: Economies in History and Theory*, New York: Free Press, pp. 64–94.

— (2001) *The Great Transformation: The Political and Economic Origins of Our Time*, 2nd edn, Boston: Beacon Press.

Priestley, Margaret (1951) 'Anglo-French trade and the "unfavourable balance" controversy, 1660–85', *The Economic History Review* 4(1): 37–52.

Rajchman, John (1985) *Michel Foucault: The Freedom of Philosophy*, New York: Columbia University Press.

Raphael, D. D. (2007) *The Impartial Spectator: Adam Smith's Moral Philosophy*, Oxford: Oxford University Press.

Rashid, Salim (1982) 'Adam Smith's rise to fame: a reexamination of the evidence', *The Eighteenth Century: Theory and Interpretation* 23(1): 64–85.

— (1990) 'Adam Smith's acknowledgments: neo-plagiarism and the wealth of nations', *The Journal of Libertarian Studies* 9(2): 1–24.

Robertson, John (1994) 'Union, state and empire: the Britain of 1707 in its European setting', in Lawrence Stone (ed.) *An Imperial State at War*, London: Routledge, pp. 224–57.

Ruffin, Roy J. (2002) 'David Ricardo's discovery of comparative advantage', *History of Political Economy* 34(4): 727–48.

Schochet, Gordon J. (1975) *Patriarchalism in Political Thought: The Authoritarian Family and Political Speculation and Attitudes, Especially in Seventeenth-Century England*, New York: Basic Books.

Schumpeter, Joseph Alois (1954a) *History of Economic Analysis*, London: Allen & Unwin.

— (1954b) *Economic Doctrine and Method: An Historical Sketch*, London: Allen & Unwin.

Schuyler, Robert Livingston (1931) 'Introduction', in Robert Livingston Schuyler (ed.) *Josiah Tucker: A Selection from his Economic and Political Writings*, New York: Columbia University Press.

Scott, H. M. (1990) *British Foreign Policy in the Age of the American Revolution*, Oxford: Clarendon Press.

Scott, Jonathan (1988) *Algernon Sidney and the English Republic, 1623–1677*, Cambridge: Cambridge University Press.

— (2000) *England's Troubles: Seventeenth-Century English Political Instability in European Context*, Cambridge: Cambridge University Press.

Seligman, Edwin. R. A. and Hollander, Jacob H. (1911) 'Ricardo and Torrens', *The Economic Journal* 21(83): 448–68.

Sharman, Jason C. (2006) *Havens in a Storm: The Struggle for Global Tax Regulation*, Ithaca, NY: Cornell University Press.

Siegel, Paul N. (1952) 'English humanism and the new Tudor aristocracy', *Journal of the History of Ideas* 13(4): 450–68.

Skinner, Quentin (1978) *The Foundations of Modern Political Thought*, 2 vols, Cambridge: Cambridge University Press.

— (1998) *Liberty Before Liberalism*, Cambridge: Cambridge University Press.

— (2002) *Visions of Politics*, 3 vols, Cambridge: Cambridge University Press.

— (2009) 'A genealogy of the modern state', *Proceedings of the British Academy* 162: 325–70.

Slaughter, Thomas P. (1984) 'Introduction', in Thomas P. Slaughter (ed.) *Ideology and Politics on the Eve of the Restoration: Newcastle's Advice to Charles II*, Philadelphia, PA: American Philosophical Society, pp. xi–xxxiv.

Sraffa, Piero (2004a) 'Note on the "Essay on Profits"', in Piero Sraffa (ed.) *The Works and Correspondence of David Ricardo*, 11 vols, Indianapolis: Liberty Fund, vol. 4, pp. 3–8.

— (2004b) 'Introduction', in Piero Sraffa (ed.) *The Works and Correspondence of David Ricardo*, 11 vols, Indianapolis: Liberty Fund, vol. 1.

Steele, Ian K. (1998) 'The anointed, the appointed, and the elected: governance of the British Empire, 1689–1784', in P. J. Marshall (ed.) *The Oxford History of the British Empire*, vol. 2: *The Eighteenth Century*, Oxford: Oxford University Press, pp. 105–27.

Stigler, George J. (1971) 'Smith's travels on the ship of state', *History of Political Economy* 3(2): 265–77.

Teichgraeber, Richard F. (1986) *'Free Trade' and Moral Philosophy: Rethinking the Sources of Adam Smith's Wealth of Nations*, Durham, NC: Duke University Press.

— (1987) '"Less abused than I had reason to expect": the reception of the *Wealth of Nations* in Britain, 1776–90', *The Historical Journal* 30(2): 337–66.

Thompson, Andrew C. (2006) *Britain, Hanover and the Protestant Interest, 1688–1756*, Woodbridge: Boydell Press.

Tribe, Keith (1978) *Land, Labour, and Economic Discourse*, London: Routledge and Kegan Paul.

— (1988) *Governing Economy: The Reformation of German Economic Discourse, 1750–1840*, Cambridge: Cambridge University Press.

— (1995a) *Strategies of Economic Order: German Economic Discourse, 1750–1950*, Cambridge: Cambridge University Press.

— (1995b) 'Natural liberty and laissez faire: how Adam Smith became a free trade ideologue', in Stephen Copley and Kathryn Sutherland (eds) *Adam Smith's Wealth of Nations: New Interdisciplinary Essays*, Manchester: Manchester University Press, pp. 23–44.

— (2005) 'Political economy and the science of economics in Victorian Britain', in M. Daunton (ed.) *The Organisation of Knowledge in Victorian Britain*, Oxford: Oxford University Press, pp. 115–37.

— (2006) 'Reading trade in the wealth of nations', *History of European Ideas* 32(1): 58–79.

Tuck, Richard (1993) *Philosophy and Government, 1572–1651*, Cambridge: Cambridge University Press.

Veyne, Paul (1997) 'Foucault revolutionizes history', in Arnold I. Davidson (ed.) *Foucault and His Interlocutors*, Chicago: University of Chicago Press, pp. 146–82.

Viner, Jacob (1937) *Studies in the Theory of International Trade*, New York: Harper and Brothers.

— (1948) 'Power versus plenty as objectives of foreign policy in the seventeenth and eighteenth centuries', *World Politics* 1(1): 1–29.

— (1976) *The Role of Providence in the Social Order: An Essay in Intellectual History*, Princeton, NJ: Princeton University Press.

Wallerstein, Immanuel Maurice (1974) *The Modern World-System. Vol. 1: Capitalist Agriculture and the Origins of the European World-Economy in the Sixteenth Century*, New York: Academic Press.

Walter, Ryan (2008) 'Governmentality accounts of the economy: a liberal bias?', *Economy and Society* 37(1): 94–114.

Watson, Matthew (2005) *Foundations of International Political Economy*, New York: Palgrave Macmillan.

Winch, Donald (1978) *Adam Smith's Politics: An Essay in Historiographic Revision*, Cambridge: Cambridge University Press.

— (1983) 'Science and the legislator: Adam Smith and after', *The Economic Journal* 93(371): 501–20.

— (1992) 'Adam Smith: Scottish moral philosopher as political economist', *The Historical Journal* 35(1): 91–113.

— (1996) *Riches and Poverty: An Intellectual History of Political Economy in Britain, 1750–1834*, Cambridge: Cambridge University Press.

Wittgenstein, Ludwig (1958a) *Preliminary Studies for the "Philosophical Investigations": Generally Known as the Blue and Brown Books*, trans. G.E.M. Anscombe, Oxford: Blackwell.

— (1958b) *Philosophical Investigations*, trans. G.E.M. Anscombe, 2nd edn, Oxford: Blackwell.

Index

For Product Safety Concerns and Information please contact our EU
representative GPSR@taylorandfrancis.com
Taylor & Francis Verlag GmbH, Kaufingerstraße 24, 80331 München, Germany

www.ingramcontent.com/pod-product-compliance
Ingram Content Group UK Ltd.
Pitfield, Milton Keynes, MK11 3LW, UK
UKHW021826240425
457818UK00006B/91